NAVI PILLAY

SAM NAIDU was born in Durban, South Africa. Currently, she is a Research Associate with the Department of English, Rhodes University, Grahamstown, South Africa. A former Commonwealth and Mellon Scholar, her research interests are postcolonial feminist aesthetics and literature of migration and diaspora. She holds a B.Journ, BA (Hons), MA and a PhD and has published extensively in her field. She lives in London with her husband, Adam, and border terrier, Leroy.

NAVI PILLAY
Realising Human Rights for All

SAM NAIDU

Arcadia Books Ltd
15–16 Nassau Street
London W1W 7AB

www.arcadiabooks.com

First published by Arcadia Books 2010

Copyright Sam Naidu © 2010

Series Editor: Rosemarie Hudson

Sam Naidu has asserted her moral right to be identified as the author of this work in
accordance with the Copyright, Designs and Patents Act, 1988.

A catalogue record for this book is available from the British Library.

ISBN 978-1-906413-45-3

Typeset in Minion by MacGuru Ltd
Printed and bound in Finland by WS Bookwell

Arcadia Books gratefully acknowledges the financial support of Arts Council England.

Arcadia Books supports PEN, the fellowship of writers who work together to promote
literature and its understanding. English PEN upholds writers' freedoms in Britain and
around the world, challenging political and cultural limits on free expression.
To find out more, visit *www.englishpen.org* or contact
English PEN, 6–8 Amwell Street, London EC1R 1UQ

Arcadia Books distributors are as follows:

in the UK and elsewhere in Europe:
Turnaround Publishers Services
Unit 3, Olympia Trading Estate
Coburg Road
London N22 6TZ

in the USA and Canada:
Independent Publishers Group
814 N. Franklin Street
Chicago, IL 60610

in Australia:
The Scribo Group Pty Ltd
18 Rodborough Road
Frenchs Forest 2086

in New Zealand:
Addenda
Box 78224
Grey Lynn
Auckland

in South Africa:
Jacana Media (Pty) Ltd
PO Box 291784,
Melville 2109
Johannesburg

Arcadia Books is the *Sunday Times* Small Publisher of the Year 2002/03

For My Mother

Contents

Introduction

*All human beings are born free and equal in
dignity and rights. They are endowed with reason
and conscience and should act towards one
another in a spirit of brotherhood.*
(Article 1. Universal Declaration of Human Rights)

WHEN NAVI PILLAY was six years old she made her
first appearance in a court of law. She was called as a
witness in a case of theft; her father had been robbed
of five rands by a conniving colleague. The thief was
found guilty but the victim, her father, was treated
disrespectfully by the police and was never recompensed (R5.00 was a large sum for a working-class
family in 1947). The experience left its mark on the
young child who somehow understood that justice
had not been served. Thus began a lifelong quest to
obtain justice and human rights for all.

❧

In August 2009 *Forbes* magazine published its list of the world's 100 most powerful women. At number sixty-four, the current United Nations High Commissioner for Human Rights, Navi Pillay, is the second African to ever make the list. *Forbes* uses two criteria to compile its list: visibility and the size of the organisation the woman heads. Navi Pillay indisputably qualifies on both scores. As the most senior UN human rights regulator, Pillay is frequently in the media spotlight, and the Office of the High Commissioner for Human Rights (OHCHR) employs about 1,000 people, wielding a budget of roughly $120 million. Pillay, who calls herself 'the voice of victims everywhere', has, according to the OHCHR mission statement, a 'unique mandate from the international community to promote and protect all human rights'.* With such enormous responsibility and far-reaching influence, Navi Pillay is without doubt an extraordinary woman whose exemplary life has its origins in one of the darkest moments in the annals of human rights and the law.

Sometimes it takes exceptional circumstances to produce an extraordinary personality. South Africa in the 1940s was on the brink of an unparalleled

---

* See the OHCHR official website http://www.ohchr.org

period in the history of human civilisation. It was the dawn of apartheid, a brutal and institutionalised system of racism. First colonised by the Dutch in the seventeenth century and then by the British in the late eighteenth century, South Africa, on the southernmost tip of Africa is rich in natural resources; a fertile, spacious, hospitable land of unsurpassed beauty. It is no wonder that European settlers flocked to this land of plenty and chose to make it their home. But the colonial process in Southern Africa was violent and unjust. As Joseph Conrad inimitably describes it, the 'conquest of the earth, which mostly means the taking it away from those who have a different complexion or slightly flatter noses than ourselves, is not a pretty thing when you look into it too much'.* The indigenous peoples of the area were enslaved, killed, disenfranchised and driven off their land. Many wars were fought between the settlers and the Africans, and even between the Dutch and British settlers themselves. By the beginning of the twentieth century the white minority population of South Africa held deeply entrenched economic and political power and the black† majority, including people of mixed race and Indian immigrants were impoverished and subjected to gross human rights

---

* Joseph Conrad, *Heart of Darkness*, p.10.
† See Glossary of Terms

violations. Worse was to follow. The formal, pervasive, and invidious system of apartheid was yet to be formally designed and implemented.

It was in this ethos, on 23 September 1941, in a suburb of Durban, in the province of Natal on the east coast of South Africa, that a baby girl was born to descendents of Indian indentured labourers. The baby, the fifth child of Narrainsamy and Santhama Naidoo was named Navanethem and she belonged to the second generation of Indians to be born in South Africa. She grew up in this fractured and inequitable society, fighting discrimination and degradation from childhood, growing evermore resolute and articulate about the role of the law in establishing and maintaining human rights in South Africa and beyond. The story of Navi's life, from her disadvantaged childhood to her appointment as UN High Commissioner for Human Rights, is a remarkable and inspirational one, which at times is breathtaking in its testimony to courage and selflessness.

The South Asian Diaspora and Indian Indentured Labourers

South Africa's turbulent history forms the backdrop to the story of Navi's life, but how did she, an ethnic Indian, come to be born in South Africa at this momentous time, when a system of such grievous injustice was being germinated? With the abolition of slavery in the vast British Empire in 1833, a new demand for cheap labour was created. British colonialists devised the Indentured Labour System, regarded by many as a glorified form of slavery. This system imposed contractual conditions upon the labourers from India who were recruited and transported to other British colonies to work mainly in sugar cane fields. Indian indentured labourers, including some of Navi's forebears, were enticed to Natal, then a British colony, with promises of a better life and assurances that their indenture contracts would protect their rights. However, the reality of plantation life in Natal was similar to the appalling experience of African slaves on American plantations. Labourers worked long hours, were flogged, jailed, denied rations and forced to live in squalid conditions. Most significantly, their only recourse, the law, was the law of the white colonists and this law did not protect or offer redress to the indentured labourers. Rather, in practice this legal system served only to consolidate the despotic power of the white colonists.*

Thus began the first wave of the South Asian diaspora. Between 1860 and 1911 about 150,000

---

* Ahswin Desai and Goolam Vahed, *Inside Indenture: A South African Story, 1860–1914*, pp.85–102.

labourers and traders migrated from Uttar Pradesh, Bihar, Tamil Nadu and Gujarat to Natal, in South Africa. Indentured labourers were also transported to Fiji and Malaysia, and the demand for sugar in the West was so huge that, during the nineteenth century, more than half a million British Indians arrived in the Caribbean.

Not all migrants during this first phase of the South Asian diaspora were labourers. In the case of South Africa, the indentured labourers were followed by traders from, first, Mauritius, and then Gujarat. Furthermore, conditions for migrants in their respective diasporic locations differed greatly according to the local politics, the specific labour conditions of that location, and the class, caste, religion and gender of the migrants themselves. For example, migrants to Malaysia later experienced the Japanese occupation of Malaysia during the Second World War, and in South Africa, migrants who decided to settle permanently were subject to anti-Indian legislation such as the Indian Immigration Law of 1895 which decreed that Indians who did not renew their indenture contracts had to pay an annual tax of £3.00 sterling. Before long, these South African Indians were to suffer further privations under the infamous apartheid regime.

Passive Resistance and the Law

Seventy years before Navi Pillay, aged twenty-four, began her career as a lawyer in Durban, another twenty-four-year-old Indian lawyer from Gujarat arrived in Durban. He had been educated at University College London and had been admitted to the British bar. Shortly after arriving in South Africa the young lawyer from Gujarat bought a first-class train ticket to Johannesburg but was ordered out of the train for being a 'coolie'.* He ended up spending an uncomfortable night at Pietermaritzburg railway station and thus began an historical career in politics and human rights. The lawyer's name was Mahatma Gandhi.

After this humiliating experience and the announcement of impending disenfranchisement laws, Gandhi decided to remain in South Africa to steer the Indian immigrant population which was growing increasingly incensed by the anti-Indian legislation aimed at curbing the Indian population in South Africa. Like Navi Pillay, who was the first black woman to establish her own law firm in South Africa, Gandhi too broke new legal-historical ground by being the first black lawyer admitted to the Supreme Court. Another remarkable similarity between these plucky young lawyers is the category of legal cases

---

* See Glossary of Terms

they became embroiled in. More than half a century before Navi Pillay began representing the victims of apartheid, Gandhi defended and secured the release of indentured labourers such as Balasundaram. It must be noted however that Gandhi's detractors are scathing about Gandhi's 'racism' – his neglect of the suffering of millions of black Africans, and his support of the British forces in the Anglo-Boer War and wars against the Zulus. The glaring difference between the two young lawyers then is that one fought for the rights of South African Indians and the other is an advocate of human rights for all.

Nevertheless, Gandhi did cut his political teeth in the ferment of race relations he encountered in South Africa. It was here in South Africa, long before he became an international icon of liberation and peace, that he first advocated a policy of passive resistance (*satyagraha*)* in the face of intractable and unjust legislation. For the entire duration of his twenty-one-year stay in South Africa, Gandhi relentlessly but peacefully marshalled the fermenting energy of the disenfranchised South African Indians: he organised strikes and marches; drew up petitions; preached a policy of non-cooperation with the white government; established a newspaper; created a communal farm on the outskirts of Durban, and was

---

* See Glossary of Terms

himself arrested on a number of occasions for civil disobedience.

In 1913 the South African government passed one of its first racist laws, the *Land Act*, which curtailed land ownership by black South Africans and forced them (eighty per cent of the population) to live in designated areas (thirteen per cent of the total land area). It was in response to such iniquitous laws that the South African Native National Congress (later the ANC) was formed in 1912. Navi Pillay's early life was deeply affected by such laws and by the atmosphere of deep dissent which prevailed in her community. Her life-story though is not one of defeat, despair or denigration. For this remarkable woman, like Gandhi, has managed to triumph where others would have given up or failed. With that rare combination of astuteness, fortitude, and clarity of vision gifted only to a few inspirational individuals, her life reads like a series of feats amidst the public and personal tribulations caused by the laws of an unjust regime.

Gandhi's endeavours in South Africa culminated in the remarkable events of 1913 when mass strike action took place across the country, and in the *Indian Relief Act* of 1914 when the government of the Union of South Africa under General Jan Smuts made important concessions to Gandhi's demands, including recognition of Indian marriages and abolition of the poll tax. Although not an unmitigated success as history shows, Gandhi left South Africa in 1914 and returned to India. He was to go on to legendarily lead India to independence from British rule. But in South Africa the situation worsened and the struggle turned violent before liberty and equality was realised almost a hundred years after Gandhi's arrival in South Africa.

Whatever his shortcomings or contradictions, Gandhi paved the way for South Africans like Navi Pillay who shared his community spirit, his sense of righteousness, and his understanding that challenging the law was a surefire way to instigate a social and political revolution. It has often been asked: where do these extraordinary people get their courage and drive from? Throughout the ages they have fought for freedom and for justice. Joan of Arc, William Wallace, Martin Luther King Junior, Nelson Mandela, Aung San Suu Kyi, the list goes on. Every epoch and every site of conflict has its heroes who work selflessly and at great peril for what might commonly be called human rights. What strikes one when perusing the annals of history is the role played by the edifice of the law in the denial or according of human rights to the diverse citizens of the world. When Gandhi, a lawyer, first encountered racism in South Africa he responded by defying the law, and then later by helping to change it. Nelson Mandela too defied the laws of the apartheid government and was imprisoned for twenty-seven years as a result. He emerged, after his period of incarceration, triumphant and able to participate in the construction of a new constitution for the country. Navi Pillay also became deeply embroiled with the law, simultaneously occupying a position within it and lobbying against it, and eventually achieving one of the highest ranks in the echelons of the international judicial system. But first she had to fight against the odds and obtain an education which would afford her the opportunity to do battle with the hydra which was the legal system of the apartheid regime.

Early Life and Education

*Everyone has the right to education ... Education
shall be directed to the full development of the
human personality and to the strengthening
of respect for human rights and fundamental
freedoms.*

(Article 26. Universal Declaration of Human Rights)

Admittance to a Segregated Education System

Navi Pillay owes her career to the chutzpah and
ingenuity of her mother who, using her own brand
of passive resistance, ensured that her daughter was
admitted to school, albeit an overcrowded and poorly
equipped one. On admittance day Mrs Santhama
Naidoo remained silent, composed and determined
whilst other mothers became irate and vociferous
because there were so few places for so many children.
In South Africa the school year begins in January and

this is the month when temperature and humidity levels soar in Durban. Imagine a small ramshackle building with the most basic of facilities and outside in the sub-tropical heat, a gaggle of anxious mothers, wilting children in tow, clamouring to be heard. In the midst of this chaos and desperation, Santhama Naidoo was calm, polite yet forceful. The school principal was so struck by her dignity that he said to her: 'You have behaved admirably and therefore I will admit your child to the school.' Mrs Naidoo then provided notebooks for Navi by stitching together the blank pages left over in her elder children's notebooks. Navi's grandfather, on the other hand, although encouraging, was concerned that Navi would write letters to boys if she learned to read and write. The virtue of the Hindu daughters was of paramount significance to the Indian immigrants whose response to cultural dislocation was to adhere ever more strongly to traditional values and customs. In contrast, her mother's words on the subject, spoken in Tamil, were to form an important mantra for her: 'You have to be educated so you will never be a slave to a man.'

For a female Indian child of working-class parents in 1940s South Africa, obtaining an education was no mean feat. Many of the girls who went to primary school with Navi had arranged marriages when they reached puberty. This was a diasporic community divided between the will to survive and flourish in a hostile adopted home, and the restrictive traditions imported from the homelands. Parents were protective of their daughters' virtue, and because a daughter owed filial allegiance to her husband's family after marriage, she did not offer future financial rewards for parents. Quite often the view held was that educating a female child was a waste and a risk. Navi's parents, through the years, were often criticised by friends and family for educating their daughters, or as the critics put it in their colourful idiom, 'Why are you pickling your daughters? You should find them husbands and get them safely married.'

In addition to such views and cultural practices, schools for black children were under-resourced and over-crowded. Black pupils often could not afford textbooks, stationery or school uniforms. As in all other areas of civil liberties in South Africa at the time, education was organised according to a strict hierarchy. White children had the best educational facilities, followed by Indian, then coloured,* and then black African children, who were given the most rudimentary education, if any at all, to secure cheap, menial labour for the white minority. This dismal state of affairs was the direct and planned outcome of the policy of 'separate development' which the South African government adopted.

---

* See Glossary of Terms

Apartheid Becomes Law

The 1940s was a rocky decade for South African politics. In 1948 the United Party, under General Jan Smuts (Prime Minister of the Union of South Africa during Gandhi's sojourn here) who was pro-British, was defeated by Afrikaner nationalists. During the South African general election of 1948 the Herenigde Nasionale Party leader, DF Malan, called for the prohibition of interracial marriages, for the banning of black trade unions and for stricter enforcement of job reservation. Running on this platform of separate development or apartheid, as it was termed for the first time, Malan and his party defeated Smuts and his United Party. The Herenigde Nasionale Party consequently became the government, renamed itself the National Party and ruled South Africa until 1994. Gandhi's worst nightmare had come true.

In 1958, a year before Navi Pillay finished secondary school, the 'architect of apartheid' as he came to be known, HF Verwoerd, became the Prime Minister. Since 1950 (incidentally, also the year that Nelson Mandela became the president of the African National Congress Youth League), he had served as the Minister of Native Affairs in the National Party government, and it was due to his meticulous blueprint that the edifice of apartheid legislation was constructed. In addition to the existing pass laws and poll taxes

which already controlled the movement and exploi-
tation of black people, more laws were passed which
were to racially divide South Africans for more than
half a century: *The Prohibition of Mixed Marriages Act*
(1949); *The Immorality Act* (1950) which banned sexual relations between whites and all non-whites; *The
Promotion of Bantu Self-Government Act* (1959) which
abolished black representation in Parliament and set
up designated 'homelands' for black Africans; *The
Bantu Education Act* (1953) which decreed that blacks
should be provided with separate educational facilities
(in practice, this law further distinguished between
Indian, 'coloured', and black African educational facilities); and perhaps most visible and risible to the rest
of the world, *The Reservation of Separate Amenities
Act* (1953) which designated that all four race groups
should have separate amenities such as train car-
riages, toilets, parks, and beaches. With the passing of
The Reservation of Separate Amenities Act thousands
of signs declaring 'Whites Only' were erected around
the country. The palace for the white minority was
ready for occupation, they took up residence within
its walls, each room a law designed to reinforce privilege, and each brick made up of the blood, sweat and
tears of the disenfranchised black majority.

Ironically, Verwoerd described apartheid as a 'policy of good neighbourliness', a term he most likely
borrowed from US President Franklin D. Roosevelt

who popularised the term during the 1930s when the USA adopted a policy of non-interventionism in its relations with Latin America. Roosevelt's policy was short-lived as the outbreak of World War Two saw neighbourly goodwill replaced by suspicion and hostility. Meanwhile, in South Africa, under the guise of 'good neighbourliness' millions of people were forced to live in poverty and squalor in the homelands whilst the strongest and the fittest were siphoned away to provide cheap labour for their gluttonous neighbour. In another wily allusive gesture, Verwoerd also declared that the blueprint for the policy of apartheid was the Indian Removal Act of the United States in the nineteenth century which saw thousands of Native Americans forcibly moved into reservations.

By some bizarre twist of fate, just as the process of formalising apartheid in South Africa began, the Universal Declaration of Human Rights (UDHR) was created. The UDHR is a declaration drawn up by the UN Commission on Human Rights as a direct consequence of World War Two. The Commission was under the leadership of Franklin D. Roosevelt's widow, Eleanor Roosevelt, and it was adopted by the United Nations General Assembly on 10 December 1948 at the Palais de Chaillot, Paris. It consists of the first global articulation of rights to which all human beings are entitled. The UDHR is made up of thirty articles which have been modified and consolidated

in subsequent international treaties, regional human rights bodies, and national constitutions and laws.*
As United Nations High Commissioner for Human Rights, it is Navi Pillay's primary task to uphold the recommendations and general spirit of the UDHR.

The laws which formed the backbone of apartheid were in stark defiance of Article 1 of the UDHR: *All human beings are born free and equal in dignity and rights. They are endowed with reason and conscience and should act towards one another in a spirit of brotherhood;* and of Article 2: *Everyone is entitled to all the rights and freedoms set forth in this Declaration, without distinction of any kind, such as race, colour, sex, language, religion, political or other opinion, national or social origin, property, birth or other status.*

Perhaps aware that the UDHR was a declaration and not a treaty and therefore not enforceable, the white minority government in South Africa propelled the wheels of the apartheid juggernaut forward, trampling the inalienable rights of millions of South Africans, and steering a due course for civil war and decades of fervent struggle.

---

* For a detailed and up-to-date account of the UDHR see Peter Halstead, *The Facts At Your Fingertips … Human Rights*, pp.24–50.

Early Promise

For Navi Pillay, the institutionalisation of apartheid formed the backdrop to her early life and education. By the time Navi reached school-going age, deep divisions in South African society were already entrenched. The odds were stacked against this precocious young woman, but her parents, Narrainsamy and Santhama Naidoo, proved to be formidable nurturers who were determined to succeed in their adopted, inequitable home. Moreover, these parents were unswerving in their ambition that their children have a better quality of life than they had had. Santhama, as already shown, was a resourceful and placid mother who instilled the value of independence and family ties in her children. Married by arrangement at the age of sixteen, she taught herself to read and write in English but was extremely well-read in Tamil. Narrainsamy, a bus driver, shared his wife's dedication to their family and is described by his youngest daughter, Jenarthenee Pillay, now a regional magistrate in KwaZulu-Natal, as '... reliable, honest, hardworking, progressive. He encouraged all his children to be strong and brave and never afraid of failure. He was so self-assured, forthright in his speech, always so confident that even though we lived in a world where we were treated as inferior, we never felt inferior to anyone. He would delight us with stories about his own father's fearlessness and physical confrontations with white police officers.'

Although Clairwood, where Navi grew up, was a relatively poor suburb with very basic accommodation, Narrainsamy built his family a six-bedroom house with the help of his wife and sons. This afforded the family of nine ample domestic space, a rare luxury at the time for a working-class family. He was protective of his daughters but markedly enlightened for his time when it came to education, and encouraged them to go to secondary school. Most of all, he wanted his children to learn self-respect and to earn the respect of others. Even at the age of 100, Narrainsamy was a man who commanded universal respect. He died in 2006 having lived through the formation of the Union of South Africa, two world wars, the introduction of formal apartheid, bloody civil strife, the eventual birth of democracy, and long enough to see his fifth child elected as a judge on the Appeals Division of the International Criminal Court at The Hague.

Navi's mother, Santhama Naidoo, died in 1979 having been the anchor in her children's lives. Although not formally educated, she would often enter into debate with her husband on political matters. Jenny recalls that as the children grew up and left home, Santhama and Narrainsamy fell into the habit of discussing interpretations of the *Ramayana* or the

*Bhagavad Gita** in the evenings. Considering Navi's outstanding achievements today, it is apparent that her parents' appreciation of education and its power to liberate, coupled with their deep nurturing spirit, and their appreciation of the significance of respect, shaped their daughter who has sought the path of self-enlightenment without abandoning a profound and practical consideration for the welfare of others.

Navi has vivid memories of the Clairwood of her childhood. She remembers that there was no water-borne sewage system. In a predominantly Indian suburb, such amenities were prohibited. She recalls that white men drove the trucks that collected the night soil (as it was euphemistically called then) and that black men carried the stinking buckets on their shoulders. The law of the land, or job reservation, ensured that employment too was organised according to a strict racial hierarchy with the lowliest positions occupied by black Africans.

One memory from Navi's childhood in Clairwood stands out. In 1952, when she was about eleven years old, she one day found herself afflicted by an excruciating toothache. A visit to a private dentist for a child of her background was unheard of in those days, so like millions of others in South Africa she went to the nearest municipal hospital and joined the

---

* See Glossary of Terms

hordes of other ailing people who had begun queuing at dawn. After a few hours of standing outside waiting to be admitted into the hospital building, the weakened child leaned against a car for a moment's respite. Immediately, the florid face of a white doctor appeared at a window. He leaned out and shouted at Navi, 'What do you think you're doing? Get away, stop leaning on my clean car!' The eleven-year-old Navi now had fear and humiliation as well as pain and exhaustion to contend with. She has never forgotten that incident.

Navi's remarkable intelligence was evident from an early age. In primary school her aptitude for learning gained her a double promotion – she was allowed to skip a year and proceed straight from Standard One to Standard Three. This early promise, nurtured by defiant parents and a close-knit community, began to burgeon a few years later when at the age of fourteen she won an essay-writing competition. The topic of the essay was 'Why we should buy South African-made goods' and her reward for this effort was the Springbok medal. Although clearly a ploy on the part of the state-controlled, separate education system to engender nationalism in the black youth of the country, Navi rose to the challenge and displayed a remarkable patriotism and sense of community, even at this tender age. When speaking about this achievement, it is clear that Navi's memory is bittersweet. She has a strong conviction that she should have been awarded a cash prize for winning the competition but for some political or racially-motivated reason, she was given just the medal. The injustices of childhood have a way of haunting one – it is up to the individual whether those harsh lessons are put to good use later in life.

Navi began her public-speaking career at about the same time. In 1956 she won the Public Speaking Contest organised by the South Coast Cultural and Educational Federation for her speech entitled 'That the individual family system is more advantageous that the joint family system'. Again this topic was a precursor to Navi's later professional concerns about family dynamics and domestic violence. A transcript of the speech was not found, but the topic is clearly controversial. Traditionally, Indian families were extended families with several generations living together under one roof. Navi's speech seems to have argued that an individual, nuclear family was the way forward. This speech was the first of many acts which were to flout convention and land Navi at the epicentre of vigorous public debate.

Navi's flair for articulating her ideas and her precocious social consciousness ensured that she would garner accolade after accolade as a teenager. She won another essay competition in 1957. This time it was a national essay competition organised by the Union of Jewish Women. Her essay topic for this competition was 'The role of women in South Africa' – a topic which was to preoccupy Navi a great deal in later years culminating in her involvement in the National Women's Coalition in post-apartheid South Africa. The Union of Jewish Women of South Africa is still active in its promotion of cross-cultural understanding and the empowerment of all South African women. When reminded of the 1957 essay competition the current Union members were amazed and tickled pink with pride that they had made a positive contribution, however small, to Navi's formative years.

A year later she took the prestigious Jan Hofmeyr trophy for public speaking. The irony of these two awards (the Union of Jewish Women essay competition and the Hofmeyr Speech Contest) is glaring to those who know only too well that white liberalism dotted the stark apartheid landscape like the threatened cycad bushes adorn the veldt.* Such cultural awards and activities added an extra dimension and complexity to race relations and political affiliations

---

* The Union of Jewish Women of South Africa was founded in 1931 by a group of affluent white women to promote Jewish culture in South Africa and to provide welfare for those disadvantaged by apartheid. Jan Hendrik Hofmeyr (1894–1948), an Afrikaner, was the Minister of Finance, the Minister of Education, and then Deputy Prime Minister in Jan Smuts's government. A fund set up after his death ran the annual Jan Hofmeyr Memorial Speech Contest in Natal.

in the 1940s and 1950s and would have been bewildering for a socially aware young woman. These liberal gestures would have seemed discordant to Navi, but she took it all in her stride, expressing her sentiments logically, passionately and with quiet zeal – signs of the germinating lawyer and human rights activist to come. She also displayed an uncanny postcolonial prescience in one so young, winning the Students' Historic Society Speech Contest in 1958 for her chosen topic: 'It would have been better for the world if Vasco Da Gama had never sailed.' But Navi was not just a bookworm and a serious thinker. She revealed her creative, flamboyant side when she played Eliza Doolittle in the school production of *Pygmalion* with much cheeky humour and high spirits.

In all of these high school pursuits Navi was spurred on by an enlightened and politically active teacher, Mr NG Moodley. Navi does not fail to pay tribute to this early mentor who was the father of Strini Moodley, a political activist, playwright and journalist who befriended Steve Biko. Strini Moodly began his activism by writing a satirical play in the early 1960s in response to the Sharpeville Massacre (an event which saw police gun down about seventy protestors in a township). He went on to become closely associated with the Black Consciousness Movement, founded by Biko, and with other radical leftist political organisations, including black theatre groups. Over the years

Strini was banned, detained and then imprisoned on Robben Island for contravening the *Terrorism Act.* Together with Saths Cooper, Strini was a flamboyant, eloquent activist who urged the Indian people to embrace Black Consciousness and unite with their fellow victims of oppression. In years to come, Navi was to be influenced by such thinking, just as much as she was inspired by her dynamic schoolteacher.

In January 1956, when Navi was ready to attend secondary school, Clairwood Indian High School, the first co-educational secondary school for Indians in Durban, had just been built. It happened that Navi was the first child to enroll at this brand new school, and for this reason, on opening day, the headmaster took her by the arm and personally led her into the building. This was an auspicious start to Navi's secondary education, especially as her admittance to primary school had been something of a struggle. Navi was a brilliant student who shone, but she was also an indigent one. When it became apparent that this young woman with immense potential could not afford the fees for higher education, the community, steered by the headmaster, VN Naidoo, rallied around her and collected the funds required. In 1959 she was the first ever pupil to be awarded the Dux Award for academic achievement at the school and it was also the year that the VN Naidoo Bursary Fund was established at Clairwood Indian High School.

Not many women from the community were that lucky. There were four girls in her matriculation class and she was the only one who made it to university.

High Education, Higher Aims

During apartheid black Africans were the most severely deprived of the three oppressed racial groups (the black Africans, the Indians and the 'coloureds'). *The Bantu Education Act* (1953)* saw to it that black Africans had the most meagre education facilities, and thus their only means of income was to work as menials for the privileged white population. When Verwoerd explained this plan to Parliament he used a paternalistic rhetoric which drew obliquely on the nineteenth-century colonialist discourses of biological determinism and ethnography:

'There is no space for him [the 'Native'] in the European Community above certain forms of labor. For this reason it is of no avail for him to receive training which has its aim in the absorption of the European Community, where he cannot be absorbed. Until now he has been subjected to a school system which

---

* This Act was consolidated in 1959 by the *Extension of University Education Act* which established separate 'tribal colleges' for black higher education.

drew him away from his community and misled him by showing him the greener pastures of European Society where he is not allowed to graze."*

Here Verwoerd is referring specifically to indigenous black Africans. But what of Indians, those migrant indentured labourers who were so determined to embrace their diasporic home? By the 1940s they were, it seems, positioned a few rungs higher on the racial hierarchy. Ever since the expiry of the first period of indenture, when Indian labourers could elect to return to India or remain in South Africa, there was a demand for formal education. Initially, white schools were open to a handful of 'free' Indians but in 1905 this 'privilege' was brought to an abrupt end. The first schools for Indians in South Africa were provided by Christian missionaries (as was the case for black Africans). One such school was St Aidan's Primary School in Durban where controversial Indian woman activist, Dr Goonam, was educated.

Dr Goonam, although a generation older, had a similar childhood to Navi Pillay. She too was outstandingly intelligent, supported in the bosom of a loving family, and subjected to the racist laws of the land. Dr Goonam's mother was educated in Tamil

---

* Peter Kallaway, *Apartheid and Education: The Education of Black South Africans*, p.92.

and her ancestors, like Santhama Naidoo's, had also migrated from India, via Mauritius. But Dr Goonam's childhood differed in one marked way – her father was a wealthy businessman who had worked his way up from a simple messenger boy and market gardener. As a teenager she did not have to fight for one of the limited places in the few Indian schools in Durban as her father could afford private tutors. Most astounding was her father's decision to send her to Edinburgh to study medicine. In her own words: 'No Indian girl remained at school once puberty set in, and the idea of sending a girl abroad was outrageous … It flouted the prevailing morals … '*

Dr Goonam returned home from Scotland in the early 1930s, the first Indian woman doctor in South Africa, to find that restrictions against Indians had worsened. In 1946, the government instituted the *Asiatic Land Tenure and Indian Representation Act* which resulted in forced removals to designated areas, and strong curtailment of property ownership and movement. Another wave of passive resistance swept through the country as thousands of Indian men and women occupied white land or held illegal meetings. Dr Goonam was a ringleader in this campaign who led thousands in marches and rallies,

---

* Dr K. Goonam, *Coolie Doctor – An Autobiography by Dr Goonam*, p.25.

and most significantly, who co-opted women into the struggle. She defied 'traditional' gender roles, reformed the elite and male-dominated Natal Indian Congress by being its first woman elected to office, and she was imprisoned on numerous occasions. Clearly, Dr Goonam was fighting a dual battle: she fought to liberate her people from the yoke of the white oppressor; and she had to fight the conventions and constrictions of the Indian community. Although a heroine to political activists, she was regarded with suspicion and prejudice by the wider community.

In very much the same way that Navi Pillay would struggle to gain acceptance as a female lawyer in Durban in the 1960s, Dr Goonam slogged to establish her medical practice in a community that believed she had no business doing a man's job. Rather than be dissuaded by these difficulties, she was spurred on to work indefatigably in various clinics across the city and to promote the rights of women; in particular, she used her influence to promote secondary education for Indian girls. Eventually, after continuous harassment from the Special Branch,* she fled South Africa and went into exile for a while in England, Australia and Zimbabwe, never ceasing to labour for her cause.

---

* See Glossary of Terms

As fate would have it, Dr Goonam was Navi's family doctor. Navi cites Dr Goonam as an inspiration and a role model, with whom she remained in contact until her death in 1999. It is not surprising that these two extraordinary women even collaborated for a while. Navi recalls that Dr Goonam offered her services when she, Navi, set up an Advice Desk for the victims of domestic abuse in the 1980s. Navi recalls with great hilarity that at one of the Advice Desk meetings, when religious leaders were consulted and one of the Hindu priests was on the podium defending the prohibition of menstruating girls lighting the holy lamp, Dr Goonam yelled, 'Where do you think babies come from? Through the ears?!'

It is not too far-fetched to infer from this connection that Navi's determination, forthrightness, and gift for steady, impassioned speech are to some extent indebted to the example set by Dr Goonam, the 'coolie' doctor, who in one of many court appearances, made the following bold declaration: 'I plead guilty and ask the court to impose the maximum sentence permitted by law ... In occupying the resistance camp I was protesting against that oppressive and pernicious law recently enacted against my people who had no part in framing it. The Act spells disaster, ruin and a state of semi-serfdom to our people who contributed greatly to the prosperity of this country. South Africa we are reminded frequently, is a democratic country ... I am here to vindicate this interpretation of democracy.'*

Dr Goonam protested against the apartheid laws and she defied the repressive gender politics of her immediate community. Navi, too, became embroiled in such a two-pronged war against discrimination and injustice. Navi's sister Dayapushnee recalls how Navi broke from the confines of a repressive society with small acts of insurgence: 'She would drive into rural areas of KwaZulu-Natal by herself, places like Marion Hill, and once her car broke down. She went to foreign countries without a chaperone, even Russia, which she explored alone. Then later when she was married, she opened her home to couples who wanted to elope – those who were seeking refuge because they were going against their families' wishes. She didn't care what people said, she helped them to marry and reconciled the families.'

In interviews Navi is often asked who her inspirations or role models were as a youth. Her responses are varied but she often mentions her forebears, the ancestors who made the journey from India across *kala pani*† to their diasporic home in South Africa. She

---

* For more on Dr Goonam see *Vocies of Resistance: Dr K. Goonam* compiled by K. Chetty: http://scnc.ukzn.ac.za/doc/Audio/VOR/ GoonamK/GoonamKbackground.htm

† See Glossary of Terms

is in awe of her grandparents who toiled on the sugar cane fields and starved themselves in order to educate their children. She mentions Dr Goonam but another name, too, crops up repeatedly, that of Fatima Meer. Fatima Meer is a highly-respected veteran of the anti-apartheid struggle. She was born in Grey Street, Durban, in 1928 to a Muslim father and a mother of Jewish and Portuguese heritage. She received her political initiation in 1946 during the Indian Passive Resistance Campaign against racist legislation, which was the biggest, most dramatic anti-government action South Africa had seen. A student of Sociology at the University of Natal at the time, Fatima established the Student Passive Resistance Committee to support the campaign. In 1949, when race riots broke out between Indian and black Africans in Durban, Fatima became involved in community work to improve relations between the factions. She did this by uniting Indian and African women under one banner – the Durban and District Women's League. She was also a founding member of the Federation of South African Women, the organisation that coordinated the famous march on the Union Buildings in Pretoria in 1956. This band of women, all of whom are recognised in South Africa today as heroines, were protesting against the *Pass Laws Act* of 1952 which stipulated that all black South Africans should carry a pass or identification document at all times.

Over the years Meer became more and more radicalised, aligning herself with the Black Consciousness Movement and the South African Student Organisation. During her life she has been banned, detained in solitary confinement, and petrol-bombed. But her resolve remained as tough as steel, and together with her husband Ismail and her son Rashid, she continued the struggle with unfaltering poise, wit, charm and elegance. Her career as an activist continues to this day, although she is now frail and wheelchair-bound.

For all these obvious reasons, Navi cites Meer as a role model. But there is another area of achievement in Meer's life which would have impressed the aspiring lawyer. Meer, too, was a pioneer in her chosen professional field. In 1956, Meer started to lecture in Sociology at the University of Natal. She was the first black woman to be appointed as a lecturer at a white South African university. She remained on the staff of the university until 1988. During her academic career she was involved in the production of about forty books, some as author, some as editor and some as publisher. She also founded the Institute of Black Research, which functioned as a publishing house and a welfare organisation. Could there be a more powerful exemplar for Navi as she embarked on *her* journey of academic excellence, professional trailblazing, and unstinting public service?

By 1959 when Navi was admitted to the University

of Natal to study for a Bachelor of Arts degree, there were a considerable number of government-aided schools for Indians in Natal, although the demand still far outweighed the supply. Crucially, a separate section of the University of Natal had been opened for black students in 1936 (thus making it possible also for Fatima Meer to attend university), due mainly to the efforts of Dr Mabel Palmer. Mabel Palmer was one of a rare breed – a white liberal who actually made practical and profound restitution to a fractured and ailing society. Palmer was born in Northumberland in the deep north of England in 1876. She was the daughter of a militant suffragette and, after studying at the University of Glasgow, the London School of Economics and Bryn Mawr College in Pennsylvania, she became an eminent economist. She settled in South Africa in 1920 and was regarded by fellow academics as a 'walking library'. Not only did she motivate for facilities for black students on the University of Natal campus, she also founded six annual bursaries for outstanding black students. Regarded, perhaps, as a bit of an eccentric by her contemporaries, Palmer also nurtured a keen academic interest in the Durban Indian population. Her book, *The History of the Indian in Natal*, was published in 1957.

Navi's high aspirations did not falter when she entered university life. She promptly made her mark by winning the Mabel Palmer Award for the best first year student at the University of Natal. The new obstacles were there to be surmounted. Navi recalls that, to the white lecturers the tiny minority of black students were invisible: 'The white lecturer never looked at the black students who sat at the back. We once brought up the black hole of Calcutta and colonial oppression, we wanted to write about our history, but he said, "You are writing with your blood," and we were not free to make our own comments.' Before finding her feet academically in this hostile environment, Navi had a setback. For the first time in her life, she failed an assignment. Eager to engage with the injustices meted out to her ancestors, Navi wrote candidly about the British occupation of India in a history assignment. Her lecturer, apparently a champion of imperialism, was unimpressed with her radical interpretation of history. Navi had failed the assignment because she did not concur with the orthodox view that the British had civilised and enlightened India.

Accompanying this denial of heritage and identity were the shabby facilities assigned to the black students. Navi good-naturedly talks of how she and her fellow students, including Justice Poswa, now a High Court judge in South Africa, were assigned to a former 'potato warehouse' in Warwick Avenue, completely separated from the main campus. She displays no rancour when she recalls their deprivations: 'We studied bills of exchange and negotiable instruments from one text-book, about thirteen of us shared that textbook.'

Undeterred and ever-buoyant, Navi continued to excel and thus self-funded the rest of her tertiary education. In 1963 she graduated with a BA, having done mainly law subjects, and was awarded the University of Natal bursary for law, but there was one major hitch. Due to a technicality of the *Extension of University Education Act* (1959), Navi was not entitled to postgraduate study at the University of Natal and so could not continue studying for an LL.B. Instead, she was being forced to transfer to a new Indian-only campus – the University College of Indians on Salisbury Island – which did not yet cater for students in the second year of their LL.B (which was the level Navi had reached). In a panic about her floundering career plans, Navi did a stint as a trainee teacher and considered her alternatives but then her fighting spirit kicked in. She wanted to be a lawyer and had worked hard towards that goal. Nothing was going to stand in her way now.

Previously, the Minister of Education had been responsible for enforcing the separate education policy, but in 1963 a Ministry of Indian Affairs was set up. Although this was clearly another manoeuvre to divide and rule, Navi realised that she had more of a chance with the new Minister of Indian Affairs who was eager to curry favour with the Indian population. Over the period of a few months she made numerous appeals to the Minister of Indian Affairs, and was eventually given special permission to continue studying at the University of Natal, but not before she was castigated by an employee at the Ministry for handwriting her correspondence. Navi still bristles with indignation when she recounts this unfair treatment, 'I did not have access to a typewriter, where was I meant to find a typewriter?' In 1965 she obtained her LL.B. in record time.

But that is not all she obtained whilst a university student. In 1959 an elfin-looking but remarkably steely Navi attended a Freshers' Ball on campus. There a fellow student called Gaby Pillay invited her to dance. Navi obliged, the young man was struck by her unconventionality, and what followed was a rocky but enduring personal and political partnership. Here Navi was defying the norm by choosing her own husband, a step Dr Goonam would have admired.* Not long after completing their respective university educations, they married in a very humble Hindu ceremony in Gaby's hometown on the north

---

* Dr Goonam herself was unmarried but had three children – a scandalous state of affairs in her milieu. She was also openly critical of forced marriages and the unnecessary expenditure of a lavish wedding.

coast of Natal. Navi describes their wedding: 'We had no jewellery, not even garlands, a small temple wedding in Stanger.' This lack of ostentation, although rare in the community, is typical of Navi who always seemed to have her eyes set on higher concerns and issues. Navi and Gaby's partnership, despite private and social adversities, lasted almost four decades.

Gaby's full name was Paranjothi Anthony Pillay. He was a tall, suave, strikingly good-looking man who had grown up in the interior of Natal – in the Hlobane mining area. As a result, his favourite food was the hard maize meal porridge that the miners ate. He spoke fluent Zulu and was an orphan. His brothers supported him in his bid for a professional occupation and he qualified as a teacher but then later re-trained as a lawyer. In the early years Navi and he shared political convictions and legal knowledge, and were thus able to work in unison against the shackles of apartheid.

Navi's youngest sister, Jenny, went to live with Navi and Gaby when she was twelve years old. She recalls that her dashing, humorous brother-in-law was different from the other men in the community – he was open and demonstrative in his affection for his wife, calling her 'Pets' and acknowledging that she was his intellectual superior (a rare occurrence in any community!). The teenaged Jenny, who was in awe of this young, dynamic couple, recalls the exciting recreational trips they took, the picnics, and the many parties they held (a pretext for political activists to gather without fear of being arrested). She feels particularly indebted to Gaby for his kind guidance and the interest he took in her education. It was Gaby who advised Jenny to study law. These were the happy days, the days when both husband and wife were struggling lawyers, the days before Navi was thrust into the limelight and onto the path of dazzling success.

The Turmoil of the 1960s

Just as Navi completed her first year of university, the ANC was banned by the South African government. For almost fifty years, the ANC had been organising marches, leading strike action, whipping up defiance against inhumane laws and agitating for the self-determination of black people. In 1946, when the NIC and TIC jointly coordinated the resurgence of passive resistance in response to the *Asiatic Land Tenure and Indian Representation Act,* it had the full backing of the ANC. A year later, the NIC and TIC signed a pact of cooperation with the ANC, and when the ANC orchestrated the Defiance of Unjust Laws Campaign in the early 1950s, many of its volunteers were SAIC members. This non-violent campaign urged non-compliance with apartheid legislation. Thousands turned out to transgress pass laws and curfew regulations or occupy 'whites only' spaces. This was Rosa Parks's defiant gesture magnified by ten thousand.

The Defiance Campaign became international news, inspiring civil rights activists in the USA and gaining the support of such leaders as India's Pandit Jawaharlal Nehru, who led a delegation to the United Nations General Assembly, requesting the UN to consider 'the question of race conflict in South Africa resulting from the policies of apartheid of the Government of the Union of South Africa'. The delegation declared that apartheid 'is creating a dangerous and explosive situation, which constitutes both a threat to international peace and a flagrant violation of the basic principles of human rights and fundamental freedoms which are enshrined in the Charter of the United Nations'. But this call for international action went unheeded.*

Nelson Mandela, a young lawyer and president of the ANC Youth League, was appointed Volunteer-in-Chief of the Campaign. He displayed outstanding leadership skills, rallying volunteers across the country, and was soon promoted within the ranks of

---

* ES Reddy, 'Defiance Campaign in South Africa, Recalled' in *Asian Times*, London, June 26, 1987.

the ANC. But the South African government retaliated with brutal force. Many, including Mandela, were arrested, parties were banned and even more severe restrictions were imposed. Yet the ANC and its allies (known as the Congress of the People) continued with peaceful means of protest, drawing up a 'Freedom Charter' for all South Africans in 1956. Mandela wrote about the Freedom Charter in an internal publication: 'For the first time in the history of our country the democratic forces irrespective of race, ideological conviction, party affiliation or religious belief have renounced and discarded racialism in all its ramifications, clearly defined their aims and objects and united in a common programme of action.'*

Like Dr Goonam, in her speech before the court that tried her for civil disobedience, Mandela focused on the principles of democracy in his discourse. However, such appeals to reason and universal morality were met with growing violence and intransigence on the part of the South African government. The world did sit up and take notice when, on 21 March 1960, a peaceful protest against pass laws in the township of Sharpeville resulted in the police opening fire on the unarmed crowd, killing sixty-nine people and

---

* Nelson Mandela, 'Freedom in our Lifetime' in *Liberation*, newspaper of the Congress Movement, June 1956.

wounding 180. The Sharpeville Massacre, one of the
darkest days in South Africa's bloody history, was
condemned by the United Nations Security Council,
and for the first time, governments around the globe
spoke out unequivocally against the police action
taken, and against apartheid. The white minority government did not back down but responded
with more ruthless and prohibiting laws. Less than
a month after the Sharpeville Massacre, the *Unlawful Organisations Act* took effect and the ANC was
immediately banned. A new era in the anti-apartheid struggle was dawning as in December 1961, the
armed wing of the ANC, Umkhonto we Sizwe (MK),
was formed.

It was in this environment of social turmoil and
political unrest that Navi Pillay persevered with her
higher education and became politicised. She joined
the New Unity Movement (NUM) mainly through
the influence of her husband-to-be, Gaby. The NUM
was an extreme leftist organisation led by intellec-
tuals who had written and disseminated theoretical
or philosophical literature on the subject of oppression. The 'armchair' activism of the NUM, as Navi
perceived it, suited the cerebral undergraduate who
was not quite battle-ready at this point. The years
ahead were to become even tougher and trickier for
Navi as her legal work was to throw her directly in
the path of high-profile members of the ANC. From

the 1960s onwards, Nelson Mandela and other ANC activists were continually arrested and brought to trial, culminating in the infamous Rivonia Trials of 1964 when Mandela was imprisoned for life. But Navi Pillay was affiliated to the New Unity Movement which began to oppose the 'softly, softly' tactics of the People's Congress, and which was to continue with its critical tirade against oppression and corruption in both the apartheid government and the post-1994 ANC government that ushered in democracy in South Africa. Was Navi Pillay, the studious and serious young woman, up to the delicate balancing act of being both a political campaigner and an advocate for human rights?

Taking On the Law

All are equal before the law and are entitled
without any discrimination to equal protection
of the law. All are entitled to equal protection
against any discrimination in violation of this
Declaration and against any incitement to such
discrimination.

(Article 7. Universal Declaration of Human Rights)

Finding a Vocation

When Navi Pillay set out as a young graduate in 1965 to find employment in the legal industry she had a good idea of what battles lay ahead. In an interview with Marguerite Guzman Bouvard, Navi Pillay described the obstacles she faced then: 'The registrar [of the University of Natal] told me there was no way he would help me find an internship because one could not have a situation where white typists had to take instructions from black persons ... I walked the city, looking for placement as an intern. All the lawyers were men, almost all white.'*

A young Indian woman, however bright and competent, had little chance of finding employment in a reputable law firm in Durban in the 1960s because the legal profession was dominated by white males. Even black male attorneys had a tough time finding employment or securing premises to practise in the city centre because according to the *Group Areas Act*, the central business district of Durban was a 'whites only' zone. Black people were not allowed into a judge's chambers and Navi has mentioned on numerous occasions that the first time she entered a judge's chambers was when she entered her own in 1994. She also recalls with wry humour that the toilets at the Durban courts were labelled 'Judges' and 'Secretaries' on the assumption that judges were always male and secretaries were inevitably female. The job-seeking Navi was in a double-bind – she was both black and female!

Besides race and gender, there was the issue of culture. As evident in Dr Goonam's struggle to establish a medical practice, there were not many Indian women professionals in Durban at the time and the

---

* MG Bouvard, *Women Reshaping Human Rights: How Extraordinary Activists Are Changing the World*, p.142.

cult of the traditional wife and mother was very much alive. So, the advent of twenty-four-year-old Navi Pillay, smart, intrepid, and articulate, raised many eyebrows but few expectations. But of course, those sceptics observing her search for her first job had not yet experienced her courage and tenacity.

Eventually, Navi found a firm that would hire her as an intern, but there was a catch. Mr NT Naicker, her first employer and the principal lawyer of the firm, was a member of the ANC and had been placed under house arrest. At the time, 'enemies of the state' or anyone under suspicion of subversive political activities could be placed under a banning order or house arrest. In effect, Mr Naicker could not leave the city of Durban, something which his job required. This meant that the young intern had to travel to the far-flung corners of the province of Natal which was largely rural, undeveloped and occupied mainly by indigenous Zulus. For Navi, it was straight into the deep end of a shark-infested legal pool, with the added challenges of indigent clients in remote locations and a language barrier.

The bulk of the work taken on by Mr Naicker's firm had to do with land and cattle disputes involving the most impoverished members of South African society. Dr Vinodh Jaichand, a South African by birth and former colleague of Navi, is now the Deputy Director of the Irish Centre for Human Rights,

Galway. He explains why black lawyers were forced to take on low-paying work: 'One of the reasons why so many black and "Indian" lawyers became activist practitioners is that they had no access to the high-fee paying commercial work, all of which went to the white firms. Many members of their community looked to the lawyer to assist them with their daily difficulties. All lawyers from the marginalised communities had a strong sense of social obligation to their communities and ran general practices with little specialisation.'*

With her highly evolved social consciousness evident throughout her years at school and university, and with this first professional appointment, it seems Navi was always destined to dedicate her life to those in dire need.

Working with an interpreter as the majority of clients were Zulu-speaking, Navi began representing the poor, often illiterate, black farmers of KwaZulu-Natal. The learning curve was steep but Navi's success rate was greater. However, she had to concede that these were small legal battles in a much bigger political war. It was at this point in her life that it became apparent to Navi that her role was not just a legal one but a political

---

* Vinodh Jaichand, 'Navi Pillay: Overcoming the Odds' in Chile Eboe-Osuji (ed), *Protecting Humanity in the Age of Navi: Essays*, [publication pending].

one, that she could not be a lawyer without being an anti-apartheid fighter. At this early juncture, whilst acting for the villagers and people under restriction orders, Navi also realised the enormity of the injustice meted out to these 'ordinary' people. She felt uncomfortable that they were forced into legal battles which entailed costs they could ill afford. Although Navi had been criticised before for not being political enough or rather, for remaining on the periphery of student politics, it is clear that at this point a political consciousness and conscience that had been kindled when still a schoolgirl, were now ignited: 'These were political offences, and this work was my grounding for the big political trials I handled later.'*

It was also at about this time that Navi formed clandestine links with Amnesty International, itself a fledgling organisation in the 1960s, and certainly not an association that Navi would have wanted to make public whilst living in a society governed by repressive apartheid laws. The relationship with Amnesty International, whose main mandate was to seek amnesty for prisoners of conscience, was to strengthen over the years but the initial connection is indicative of Navi's widening scope of interest, and indeed, even today she claims that her heroes and influences were never restricted to her immediate milieu. When

---

* MG Bouvard, p.144.

questioned about role models and influences on her life, Navi does acknowledge someone like Mahatma Gandhi, whose dignity in the face of brutality helped her face the daily humiliations of apartheid. But she is vociferous about the diverse backgrounds of her role models and the varied influences on her life. She declares quite emphatically that Indians did not have only Indian heroes. Regarding herself first and foremost as a South African (thus putting national identity above ethnicity), she sought help and advice from near and far in her quest for justice.

In 1967, two years after securing her first job and on the day she was admitted to the bar, Navi opened her own law practice. By taking this momentous step Navi was making history. She was the first black woman in Natal to open her own practice and one of the few black women lawyers in the whole country. Navi had decided that if the world could not accommodate her, she was going to change the world, whatever the obstacles. Money was tight for the newlyweds, Navi and Gaby, so Navi's father, Narrainsamy Naidoo, the former bus driver, loaned her the capital to start the practice (he had acquired the money through the sale of his house).

Navi Pillay & Partners was more than a law practice – this was a family enterprise which employed husband Gaby, brother Gan for twenty-eight years, niece Kanthy, friend Sonny Venkatrathnam, and youngest

sister Jenny, aged thirteen, was hired first to compile a scrap book on treason trials, and again in 1979
when she too qualified as a lawyer and needed that
first break. Having been given this break, Jenny, in
1992, made history when she became one of the first
two black persons in South Africa to be appointed as
a Regional Court Magistrate by the Department of
Justice.

Those early years, as an up-and-coming lawyer
with her own practice, are recalled fondly by Navi.
She remembers that for each one of the detractors
who thought her presumptuous for starting her own
firm, there were those who supported her and sent
work her way. She is still struck by the camaraderie
she and Gaby shared with the black lawyers in Durban at the time. The *Group Areas Act* had chopped
up the city into segments – the central business
district was for white lawyers; there was an Indian
enclave around Grey Street, and then further afield,
on the outskirts of the city, the black African lawyers
were allowed to practice law. Gaby, as a favour to his
black African colleagues, signed the lease for three
premises closer to the central business district. The
landlords were aware of the duplicity, but they turned
a blind eye, and soon Navi and Gaby had a network
of like-minded compatriots of various backgrounds
who pooled resources and bolstered morale.

One of Navi's first cases as her own boss was to

defend ANC member Phyllis Naidoo who was under banning orders. Phyllis Naidoo, now a well-known name in South African households, was a young sari-clad wife, mother and student then. She was first banned in 1966, and then placed under house arrest. A decade later in 1977 (the year that Steve Biko was murdered by the South African police), she went into exile and only returned after Mandela was released in 1990. In addition to her own privations, Phyllis Naidoo's husband was imprisoned on Robben Island for five years and one of her sons was murdered on an ANC farm in Lusaka. In 2003, she was awarded the Order of Luthuli, an award for her contribution to the liberation struggle.

At the time that Navi befriended her, Phyllis Naidoo was a law student with two children and a husband in prison. She had no money for the legal fees and Navi compassionately, and because she considered herself to be inexperienced, offered to defend her *pro bono*. But the magistrate and the prosecutor were unyielding and Phyllis was sentenced to a year's imprisonment, which fortunately was suspended to seven days. Still, Navi felt responsible for Phyllis, especially as she was aware of how ghastly the conditions were in prisons for black persons and she knew what stress Phyllis was already suffering. For Navi this was clearly not just work, this was her heart and soul. Despite the setback, her ability to empathise with her clients made her evermore determined to see justice served and human rights upheld.

Meanwhile to establish her practice Navi took on all sorts of work, that is, all sorts of work available to her as a black lawyer. She was not picky or partisan, but there is a common thread to this grassroots legal work. 'I did everything. I did criminal work. I did civil work. I did estates and trusts. I did ordinary common-law crimes, but everything was political. I acted for students and trade unionists. I acted for members of all political groups in South Africa ... Without even me choosing, my work immediately became focused on human rights.'*

A glance at this early stage in Navi's career reveals an emerging common theme. Navi was immersed in the harsh realities and everyday lives of the victims of apartheid. She herself was under enormous risk of falling victim to the repressive laws of the land. But she did not flinch or baulk at the challenges a totalitarian regime created for her. Rather we see the seeds of a personal philosophy germinating: Navi was not swayed by party politics but rather she was galvanised into action by the rights of the individual. In later years this non-partisan, humanitarian stance was to win her admiration as well as criticism.

---

* MG Bouvard, p.145.

Treading a Fine Line

In 1971, Gaby and other New Unity Movement (NUM) members were detained under the *Terrorism Act*. This Act gave the state unlimited power to detain countless men, women and children for indefinite periods of time, to imprison them in solitary confinement, and to interrogate them. It also prohibited the courts from ruling on the validity of the detentions or granting any *habeas corpus* relief.* In recent years, Navi has described this Act as being modelled on the UK *Terrorism Act* targeting the IRA. Gaby and his cohorts were held in isolation in various police stations around the province. Navi went into action.

Her decision to represent Gaby as well as the other prisoners in his group was to lead her into very dangerous terrain as now she was in direct conflict with the state. Together with Gaby, Navi was a member of the New Unity Movement, as was their close friend, Sonny Venkatrathnam. Navi, however, did not make her membership known and neither was she actively involved in the NUM's covert operations. She was focused rather on representing victims of an unjust legal system. Navi was no longer an 'armchair' activist.

---

*Navanethem Pillay, 'Equal Justice for Women: A Personal Journey', *Arizona Law Review*, Volume 50, Number 3, Fall 2008 p. 659.

In an interview, Sonny recalls how brave Navi was to act as their instructing attorney: 'Navi virtually gave up her practice to represent us. She was unflinching in her devotion to the task and being outside of politics helped her deal with the counsellors. She had the ability to stand back and look at the bigger picture.' For Navi the 'bigger picture' was the rights of these prisoners of conscience. Sonny's perspective is that Navi was rather inexperienced, in a legal sense, when she took on this case but that she learned quickly, travelling to gather evidence for the defence and appearing in court every day. But yet again Navi lost the trial and the more serious offenders such as Sonny, and Kader Hassim, a lawyer himself, were sentenced to imprisonment on Robben Island. Remarkably this was not the outright defeat it appears to be at first glance. In fact, this trial heralds one of Navi's first major legal victories. Rather than wringing her hands in despair at the predicament of her husband, she utilised his power of attorney to bring an action in his name asking the courts to order his protection from torture in custody.

What in effect she had done was to make to the Supreme Court of South Africa an application against torture, or in other words, an application to stop the police from using unlawful methods of interrogation. Affidavits from other detainees recounting torture and ill-treatment were filed in support of

the application. During this landmark legal procedure Navi was advised by a well-known Jewish lawyer at the time called Rowley Arenstein, a man she
describes as 'a real doyen in the struggle'. In later years
Navi was to be criticised for working with Arenstein,
a white man, and her detractors accused her of 'con-
sorting with collaborators'. Perhaps this criticism is
the reason Navi is indignant when questioned about
her role models. In the South African context Navi
was not a conventional left-wing activist – she sought
aid and advice from anyone who shared her values,
regardless of race, ethnicity, religion or class. Rowley
Arenstein and his wife Jacqueline did indeed have a
very different upbringing from Navi but they were
leading members of the South African Congress of
Democrats and the South African Communist Party.
Rowley defended black political activists and Jacqueline was herself a defendant in the infamous Treason
Trials of 1956. Jacqueline also served on the executive
of the South African Indian Congress. Over the years
both husband and wife were imprisoned under the
Suppression of Communism Act, and were banned or
placed under house arrest.

With Rowley's assistance, Navi's application to the
Supreme Court was successful. The court ordered
the police to refrain from using unlawful methods of
interrogation on Gaby and to serve the order on him
even though he was in solitary confinement. Navi

Pillay had made the first successful challenge against the *Terrorism Act*, setting a precedent which was to have far-reaching effect. In 1972, the United Nation's Subcommittee of the General Assembly on apartheid adopted the application as a document in their collection on torture.

The Robben Island Connection

But the defence *did* lose the case and for Navi there were also personal consequences. She was now within the radar of the security apparatus of the apartheid state. Many years later, in 1997, the Truth and Reconciliation Commission (TRC) uncovered a list of 'politically-sensitive' activists compiled by the apartheid government's State Security Council. The names on the list were targeted for varying degrees of censure by the state. Navi was on that list, deemed a danger to the state, and she was therefore denied a passport for several years. She and Gaby were also under surveillance for many years.

Characteristically, Navi was undeterred. In 1972 she decided to appeal the sentence, and this is how Navi got to visit the most notorious prison in recent history. By then Nelson Mandela had been on Robben Island for almost eight years and the prison had become a symbol for human rights abuses the world over. A decade before the NUM members were arrested, Mandela had been arrested and tried for sabotage, treason, and plotting a foreign invasion of the country. These were capital crimes. From the dock Mandela defended the ANC's use of violence, saying that the ANC had deployed peaceful means to challenge apartheid until the Sharpeville Massacre. Mandela was familiar with the machinations of the South African legal system having opened a law practice in Johannesburg with Oliver Tambo in 1952. During what became known as the Rivonia Trial, Mandela made a statement about his cause. This much-quoted statement has now become immortalised as Mandela's most succinct and powerful declaration of purpose: 'During my lifetime I have dedicated myself to the struggle of the African people. I have fought against white domination, and I have fought against black domination. I have cherished the ideal of a democratic and free society in which all persons live together in harmony and with equal opportunities. It is an ideal which I hope to live for and to achieve. But if needs be, it is an ideal for which I am prepared to die.'*

Historians have also compared these words to Martin Luther King Junior's 'I have a dream' speech

---

* For a full transcript of the speech see http://www.anc.org.za/ancdocs/history/rivonia.html

which was delivered about a year before Mandela's address to the court.

The outcome of the Rivonia Trial was that Nelson Mandela and six others were sentenced to life imprisonment for treason. Thus they were sent to Robben Island, a maximum security prison for political prisoners about eleven kilometres off the coast of Cape Town. Since colonial times the island has been used as a prison and as a place of banishment for lepers and the mentally ill. Today Robben Island, which provides a focal point for South Africa's complex heritage, houses a museum and is a world heritage site. Of the twenty-seven years of his life sentence that Mandela served, eighteen were spent on Robben Island.

Sonny Venkatrathnam who spent six years on Robben Island describes conditions there for 'terries' – those prisoners who had contravened the *Terrorism Act*: 'All Afrikaner wardens hated the "terries". We had no paper, no stationery, no access to the library. There were 200 people to one large cell; we had only a mat and a blanket. Sometimes we were thrown into isolation and no reasons were given. We had to do hard labour in the quarries, it was bitterly cold on the island and everything tasted of sea salt.' A political prisoner deemed more dangerous, as Mandela was, was kept segregated in a small cell with a mat for a bed and a bucket for a toilet.

For Sonny the prospect of years in prison without

any literature to read and study was untenable. He had braced himself for the other privations and torments, but he could not imagine years of such agony without the respite of a good read. He devised a plan. He had brought to the island one book – *The Complete Works of William Shakespeare* – thinking that this text would provide the most and best quality entertainment. Knowing full well that the book would be confiscated by the wardens of Robben Island, he cleverly disguised it as a holy book of Hindu scripture by pasting onto its cover and spine Diwali* cards he had received from friends and family. These cards depicted colourful Hindu deities. When questioned by the Afrikaans-speaking warden, Sonny claimed that this was his 'bible'. Aware that the wardens were almost all staunch Christians who respected little else in their prisoners but a sense of religiosity, Sonny knew that with this deception he would be able to keep the proscribed book. That is how the 'Robben Island Bible' came into existence. The text was passed around between the inmates and still reveals the marks made by those toil-hardened hands. It also bears the signatures of many of Sonny's comrades. Today Sonny keeps this treasured memento safe in a lined box, where perhaps he also stores his nightmarish memories of those years on Robben Island.

---

* See Glossary of Terms

Sonny and his fellow inmate Kader Hassim insti-
gated a petition demanding basic human rights for
these prisoners. A copy of the petition was handed to
the Officer Commanding of the prison and another
copy was given to Navi Pillay (as Sonny and Kader's
attorney she was allowed to visit them in prison) who
smuggled it off the island. With the help of Sonny's
wife Theresa, Navi brought an application based on
this petition before the Supreme Court in Cape Town.
The judge found in favour of the prisoners. Theresa
Venkatrathnam and Navi had also alerted Amnesty
International to the plight of prisoners in South African prisons. In 1972, conditions for all prisoners on
Robben Island, including Nelson Mandela, changed.
For the first time they had access to libraries and recreational facilities, were given proper food, and most
significantly, they now had the right to proper legal
procedure and legal representation. Navi Pillay had yet
again taken on the apartheid state and she had won.

But the war was far from over and many more battles needed to be fought. Before the end of the 1970s
she was to become embroiled in another high-profile
political case. In 1978, she acted as the defense attorney
for Harry Gwala, leader of the ANC for Natal Province, and nine other ANC members charged under
the *Terrorism Act*. This was a drawn-out and compli-
cated case in which the prisoners testified to police
torture and ill-treatment. Navi was convinced that

testimony was extracted from these prisoners under duress. Previously, when acting for Kader Hassim and Twelve Others, she consulted with an eminent psychiatrist, Dr Louis Jolyon West, from the University of California, Los Angeles, to provide expert evidence on Depression, Dependence, and Debility Syndrome and its effects on detainees kept in confinement for long periods of time. But then the judge refused to hear the testimony of the expert witness. Now, when defending Harry Gwala, Navi found that the state had based its case on the evidence given by another ANC member, who according to his wife, had been brutally beaten and forced to make a statement against his comrades. Once more Dr Louis Jolyon West, who had been a consulting psychiatrist in the Patty Hearst trial, was consulted and he testified that there was a tendency for detainees to want to please their interrogators. While the court accepted the expert evidence as authoritative, it dismissed the defence's argument that evidence of the detainees was inherently unreliable.*

Once more Navi lost the case but not the battle for justice. All of the accused were sentenced to imprisonment on Robben Island, five of them including Harry Gwala received a life sentence. Her clients did not reproach her, rather they encouraged her to disseminate the information she had gathered. Nevertheless,

---

* Navanethem Pillay, p. 660.

by involving such an eminent, international scholar, Navi had succeeded in increasing global awareness of the human rights abuses taking place in South African prisons. With the recent Soweto Uprising (1976) and Steve Biko's murder (1977) still fresh topics in the international media, the time was ripe for further action and more exposure.

Ever since the Sharpeville Massacre of 1960, South Africa was internationally condemned for its apartheid regime. In addition, due to the pressure exerted by a broad coalition of organisations (black and civil rights, churches, trade unions, and students), a campaign for economic disengagement from South Africa was in place. After the Soweto Uprising the international response to apartheid grew more vociferous and unequivocal. On 16 June 1976 about 20,000 schoolchildren marched in protest against a decree by the Department of Bantu Education that Afrikaans had to be used as one of the languages of instruction in secondary schools. A few hours into the march the police opened fire and unleashed their dogs on the unarmed children. This act of police brutality was to spark a wave of violence which spread across the country and lasted almost a year as incensed black people in townships clashed with the police and the state's anti-riot unit. In a week 176 lives were lost, including two white administrators, and within a year more than 600 died.

Leading authority on African liberation struggles, George Houser, assesses the response of the United Nations to this catastrophic chain of events:

> 1976 was a landmark session for the General Assembly on southern Africa. Thirty-seven resolutions were passed by overwhelming majorities marking the year of Soweto and Transkei 'independence'. There was the World Conference for Action against Apartheid in 1977, and the Seminar on South Africa's Military Build-up and Nuclear Plans held in London in 1978. The year beginning on 21 March 1978 was also proclaimed and observed as International Anti-Apartheid Year. [...] The resolutions of the General Assembly annually called for the isolation of South Africa, for a boycott of South African goods and for sanctions. [...] The Security Council was more inhibited in its action than the General Assembly because of the constant reality of veto against any move for sanctions on South Africa by the three Western Permanent Members of the Security Council.*

In principle at least the United Nations General Assembly denounced the actions of the South

---

* George Houser, The International Impact of the South African Struggle for Liberation. http://www.anc.org.za/ancdocs/history/misc/hous123.html

African government, but in effect, the outside world was dithering in its actions against apartheid. It fell to the stalwart organisations and fearless individuals like Navi to keep up their efforts against the might of the unjust few who wielded power.

Personal Crises

Whilst the country was plunged into chaos and strife and international sanctions and embargos threatened the economy, Navi faced very personal trials. Navi and Gaby were not able to have children of their own and Navi's gruelling schedule began to take its toll on her health. The arduous cases Navi had undertaken and their restricted living conditions (they rented a small outbuilding for the first years of their marriage, and they were constantly under police surveillance) contributed to her stress and inability to conceive. In addition the Pillays did not earn very much money. Due to the fact that many of their clients could not afford legal fees, Navi and Gaby took on many *pro bono* cases. Sometimes their grateful clients paid them in kind, and in a few extreme instances, the compassionate couple ended up buying goods from their clients who were struggling peddlers or hawkers. As a result their humble household sometimes had a surfeit of towels or baked goods!

Both Navi and Gaby longed for a family but it was Navi who suffered terribly from feelings of failure and dissatisfaction. She also underwent nineteen surgical operations during this time but to no avail, so eventually a decision was made. After seven years of marriage the couple decided to adopt. Fortunately, Navi's close friend, Theresa Venkatrathnam (wife of Sonny), introduced the couple to a social worker who was able to assist and advise the couple. In due course, two much-anticipated daughters, Isvari and Kamini, were adopted. The girls were adopted at birth, first Isvari in 1973, and then Kamini in 1976. Navi's private ambition to be a mother was fulfilled.

Yet dark clouds loomed over another area of her private life. Gaby and Navi worked alongside one another for many years but this partnership was not a complete success. It became more and more apparent with time that Gaby was an alcoholic and as Navi's career soared, his flagged. As can be expected, Navi Pillay did not allow personal heartache or private tensions to negatively affect her work. Although bitterly disappointed by her failure to exonerate the political activists she had defended, Navi remained determined, focused and hopeful. Perhaps her saving grace at this stage of her career was the insight she had into her own untenable position in the South African judiciary: 'I realised that I was deluding people into thinking that there was such a thing as achieving justice in our court system.'*

Achieving justice is what drove Navi. She was not about to give up on this deep-seated conviction, and so she turned her mind and her will to revolutionising the South African legal system.

The Harvard Years

In the early 1980s, Navi began to realise that perhaps her battles needed to be fought on a different stage. Although she was a member of the Civil Rights League and of Lawyers for Human Rights Association, and had been successful, to a degree, in reforming the South African judicial system, the system was still warped and she felt strait-jacketed. With its raft of repressive laws, the system was an aberration which stripped Lady Justice of her blindfold and scales and left her wielding a viciously sharp sword. Former colleague and close friend, Durban attorney, Zubie Seedat, confirms that the iniquitous laws and apparatus of apartheid had a profound effect on Navi, as they did on all those of her ilk. When Navi saw an advertisement for a scholarship in a newspaper she saw her chance. In her own words: 'I wanted an opportunity

---

* MG Bouvard, p.153.

to expose these cases and to study the reliability of evidence taken from detainees. It's because of what Harry Gwala and the others had said that I applied for the Harvard South Africa Scholarship.'*

Navi added the Harvard South Africa Scholarship to her long list of awards and achievements and in 1981, taking her elder daughter, Isvari, who was now eight years old, with her, she travelled to Cambridge, Massachusetts, to study for an LL.M. or Master's degree in Law. After they had settled into their apartment, Isvari was enrolled into a local school and into after-school care, where the prospect of not wearing a uniform compensated for the sadness she felt at having left her younger sister at home. Navi also missed the six-year-old Kamini, who had just started her first year at school in Durban, but Navi was by now a woman accustomed to making sacrifices in order to pursue her dreams. Anyway, Kamini was well cared for by Gaby and the trusted housekeeper Beatrice Boniwe Hlope who had joined the Pillay family in about 1979 and who remained in their employ for thirty years. Like millions of other black African women in South Africa, Beatrice was not educated or trained for any vocation. To make a very modest living she left her home and family at the St Faiths mission station in rural KwaZulu-Natal

---

* MG Bouvard, p.153.

to find employment as a domestic worker in the city. She proved to be of invaluable assistance as a house-keeper and child-carer to the ambitious, hardwork-ing Navi. With some input also from grandfather Narrainsamy, Kamini was not too perturbed by the absence of her mother and sister.

At Harvard, Navi was able to focus freely on what was closest to her heart: human rights, women's rights and labour issues. And here for the first time she engaged with the internationally accepted norms of free and fair trials. The move to the USA constituted an intellectual re-awakening for Navi. In this context of constant debate and free speech she was stimulated into seriously pursuing her interest in international law. In her discussions with fellow legal academics she was able to present the case of Harry Gwala as an example of South Africa's corrupt judicial system. Perhaps Navi was motivated also by a sense of guilt at having lost the Gwala case. As a form of recompense for losing the case, Navi had made a promise to Harry Gwala and his cohorts to publicise the fact that politi-cal prisoners in South Africa were beaten and tortured. At Harvard Navi grabbed the opportunity to do this.

She spoke to many experienced judges, includ-ing the prominent African-American judge, Leon Higginbotham, who declared that Harry Gwala would never have been convicted in an American court, based on the evidence that witnesses had been tortured. Higginbotham, a civil rights advocate and a federal appeals court judge, was a giant in the USA's legal sphere. During the 1960s he had served as an adviser to President Lyndon Johnson after the assassination of Martin Luther King Junior and also after the assassination of Robert Kennedy. A canny player when it came to race relations and the laws of a society in transition, Higginbotham proved to be extremely helpful to South Africa as it transformed into a democracy. He founded the South Africa Free Election (SAFE) fund, which raised millions of dollars for the first democratic elections held in April 1994, serving also as an international mediator for this landmark process. Later he was involved in the drafting of South Africa's new constitution. As a Professor at Harvard, the great man not only taught Navi but also supervised her thesis.

Navi Pillay was not the only South African lawyer to benefit from Higginbotham's formidable body of knowledge and experience. In 1986–87 Higginbotham's clerk was Sandile Ngcobo, later Chief Justice of the Constitution Court of South Africa. Since August 2009, Ngcobo holds the office of Chief Justice of South Africa. What Navi learned from these encounters with legal boffins is that she had to change her tactics. She realised that she had to deploy human rights arguments, introduce natural justice, and cite international conventions in order to ensure a free trial. But the time for such a rehabilitation of the South African judicial system had not yet arrived.

The studious Navi also seems to have relished the ethos of scholarship at Harvard. She produced two significant papers in that busy year: 'Change in South Africa through Black Trade Unions', and 'Police Misconduct' – a paper which emerged from fieldwork conducted for her course on Public Interest Litigation: Race and Poverty. Navi had travelled a long way from the land and cattle disputes she had tackled as an intern in rural Natal and now she was closer to her goal of understanding how justice may be acquired for the millions of disenfranchised people in her homeland. At this juncture, in 1981, Navi's research convinced her that the main impetus for change in South Africa would come from the protest activities of the trade unions, coupled with the pressure exerted by sanctions. There is also the strong possibility that Navi's views in this respect were influenced by her father, Narrainsamy Naidoo, who was a co-founder of the Bus Employees' Union, and a trade unionist all his working life. History reveals that Navi was not far off the mark, though, of course, it is widely held that the escalating violence during the 1980s is what brought the white government to its knees.

The year spent in the USA was a great eye-opener and stimulus for Navi. It seems a logical progression then that after being awarded an LL.M., Navi returned to Harvard in 1984 to enroll for an S.J.D. (doctorate in juridical science). This time she funded the endeavour herself and took both her daughters with her. Navi was fortunate to be appointed as the warden of a student residence, Eliot House, so the family of three was comfortably ensconced in a temporary home on the Harvard Law School campus. For Isvari, and Kamini in particular, the most exciting thing about their amazing American adventure was that the school they attended was multiracial and multinational. The principal of the school was African-American! Imagine their delight and bewilderment at being able to interact freely with children of diverse backgrounds. Although their parents' political activism meant their home was open to people of all races, they had attended racially segregated schools in South Africa, and this was the mid 1980s, a time of violent civil unrest when relations between South Africa's race groups were most tense and volatile.

The main reason for this heightened strife was the introduction of a new constitution by the Prime Minister, PW Botha. In 1983, Botha had created the Tricameral Parliament. Two new houses of parliament were added to the whites-only House of Assembly: the House of Representatives for 'coloureds'; and the House of Delegates for Indians. Theoretically the 'coloureds' and the Indians were now enfranchised, but in effect the whites still held legislative power. No concessions were made to the majority black African population. Botha declared himself State President under this new-fangled constitution. In retaliation to growing dissatisfaction from the black Africans who remained unrepresented and downtrodden, Botha increased security measures by declaring a national state of emergency and intensifying covert operations against political activists. Navi no doubt kept track of events back home with growing trepidation, but the girls, in their 'rainbow' classroom, were blissfully unaware of the forces that were tearing their homeland apart.

Navi's response was to write a controversial thesis. Her doctoral thesis topic was 'The political role of the South African judiciary'. The gist of her argument was that as long as a judge implemented unjust, immoral laws, he/she could not fulfill their role as a judge. Again Navi's purpose is resolute: the monstrous machine that had destroyed the lives of thousands of civilians and mired her efforts as an attorney was now her intellectual opponent – the law student was taking on the South African judicial system once more. One tactic which worked well for Navi now (and had done so in the past) was that her research topic generated a great deal of discussion and interest. She was able to cajole high-profile judges in the USA and leading academics in the field to join the debate about South Africa. One such academic who

Navi cites as a major influence is the Felix Frank-
furter Professor of Law at Harvard, Alan Dershowitz,
who is also renowned as a lawyer, jurist and political commentator. Another matter of grave concern
to Navi, the psychological effects of incarceration on
prisoners, was explored and discussed during this
time, usually in the lectures of Professor Alan Stone,
the Touroff-Glueck Professor of Law and Psychiatry.
During both of her postgraduate programmes at Harvard, Navi tried to expand her legal knowledge base
by taking courses on family law, law and psychiatry,
law and economic change, and law of indigenous
populations. With this knowledge as ammunition,
Navi was ready for battle.

Navi and the girls returned to an increasingly turbulent South Africa in 1985. The country was riven by
violence, the effects of economic sanctions, and internal conflicts as frustrated political factions turned
against one another. Navi was deeply affected by the
suffering of her countrymen and women, and by the
brutality of the regime. Yet Navi was optimistic, sens-
ing that change was inevitable. She remained focused
on what for her was the most effective weapon against
apartheid – the overhaul of an immoral judicial system. To this end she also became deeply involved in
community-based activism and legislative reform on
a national level. Keeping many irons in the fire, the
resolute Navi also researched and wrote furiously for

two years. It helped a great deal that the Natal Law Society awarded her a bursary for postgraduate study in 1988 so that she could complete the write-up of her thesis.

When Navi graduated with an S.J.D. in 1988 she was the first South African to be awarded this degree from Harvard. Although her achievement was duly noted, the actual subject matter of the thesis did not receive attention from the media or scholars in South Africa. In 1988 her topic was still far too inflammatory. Later, in the 1990s, when the South African legal system was revised under the auspices of the Minister of Justice, Dullah Omar, Navi's thesis was a key reference text. It is humbling to note that Navi was not happy to just personally reap the rewards of a Harvard education. It was not long before she joined the selection committee of the Harvard South Africa scholarship programme so that she could facilitate the legal careers of other outstanding fellow citizens.

There was achievement too on the personal front. Navi was extremely courageous and unorthodox when she first decided to take up the Harvard South Africa scholarship. In addition to all the other considerations such an uprooting necessitated, she had a very tough decision to make regarding her family. At the risk of causing deep or lasting ructions she split up the family taking, first, one daughter, and subsequently both daughters away from their father, friends, family and familiar surroundings, for what ostensibly seemed like a career move. For this Navi would have received strong condemnation from a community which still predominantly believed that a woman's primary role was as wife and mother. Perhaps after her sojourns in the USA, Navi realised more than ever the burdens of her gender. But never one to kowtow to conventions, she had also during the course of the years encountered women like Phyllis Naidoo, Dr Goonam and Fatima Meer who combined a sense of civic duty and the responsibilities of motherhood with grace and fortitude. Navi, at this point in her life, joined this rank of women who paradoxically go against the status quo whilst somehow managing to fulfill one of the most universal of occupations – that of mother.

For Navi the Harvard years were a springboard to the international arena. Not only was she exercising her intellectual muscles in an institution that fully recognised her status as a human being and could therefore nurture her formidable mind, she was also making contacts in the wider arena of human rights activism. In the early 1990s after returning to South Africa and with a network of international connections in place, Navi began attending international conferences on human rights. Some of her first experiences of international human rights lobbying took place at the Conference for Women's Rights in

Asmara, Eritrea; National Union of Eritrean Women and Fund for Peace in New York; the Regional Workshop on Reproductive Rights and Population Policy in Nairobi, Kenya; the Conference on Health and Population Policies, Rio de Janeiro, Brazil; the World Conference on Human Rights, Vienna, 1993; the International Conference on Population and Development, Cairo, Egypt; and the African Regional Conference on Women, Dakar, Senegal. During this whirlwind period of two years Navi travelled around the globe to deliver papers and to participate in discussions, thus establishing herself as a world authority on human rights issues. Although unaware of career opportunities to come, Navi was laying down the groundwork for a future in the highest echelons of international human rights advocacy.

On a somewhat different tack to her usual courtroom battles and tedious processing of reams and reams of legal data, Navi was invited in 1988 to join the Amnesty International Human Rights Now! concert tour to commemorate the fortieth anniversary of the Universal Declaration of Human Rights, the document which Verwoerd had so patently disregarded. Navi accompanied musicians such as Bruce Springsteen, Tracy Chapman, Peter Gabriel, Sting, and Youssou N'Dour on this world tour. These stars had offered their services for free to Amnesty International and Navi declared in a newspaper article that they 'were interested in music to communicate their messages of peace, love and friendship ... Contrary to their glamorous images, they are really interested in singing for a cause.'* But Navi was not just on the tour for the ride. She managed to convince Amnesty International to adopt South African prisoners as prisoners of conscience and Navi was one of the informants who sent suppressed information to Amnesty International about prisoners and children in detention.

This tour also saw the cementing of a friendship and professional association which has led to a formidable duo in women's rights activism. Jessica Neuwirth was one of the organisers of the Amnesty International Human Rights Now! concert tour. Four years earlier, Jessica Neuwirth went to Durban on a Harvard Law School Human Rights fellowship to work as Navi's intern. During her six weeks in South Africa, whilst helping with research, Jessica discovered the unique combination of 'legal creativity, political skill, and personal determination'† which Navi was endowed with. At the time Navi was involved in an appeal on behalf of a group of children in the Orange

---

* Sharon Chetty, 'Durban's Navi and the Rock Superstars' in *The Sunday Times Extra*, 6 November 1988, p.10.
† Jessica Neuwirth, 'Navi Pillay: Up Close and Personal' in Chile Eboe-Osuji (ed), *Protecting Humanity in the Age of Navi: Essays* [publication pending].

Free State* who had been tortured in detention. Jessica developed a deep respect for her mentor when she learned that Navi had 'introduced into South African jurisprudence a concept developed by Dr Louis Jolyon West in the context of North Korea, that prolonged incommunicado detention undermin[es] the credibility of any statements made by those subjected to it.'† Navi, of course, ever since 1971 when she first became directly cognisant of the brutal means South African police used to extract evidence from detainees, was indefatigable in her crusade to put an end to the torture of prisoners.

Later, this respect for Navi's commitment to human rights issues was to take a very definite path when Jessica found herself being educated by Navi on the subject of women's rights. In 1992 Navi wrote: 'We see women's rights as human rights because women have been systematically disadvantaged as a group. Only the male perspective has been validated as the norm, in literature, law, and the religion.'‡ Critics may view Navi's conflation of women's rights and human rights as simplistic, but Navi was never one to mince her words. She was tired of seeing women's rights

---

* See Glossary of Terms
† Jessica Neuwirth, [publication pending]
‡ Navanethem Pillay, 'Equal Rights for Women', in *African Law Review*, 3 April 1992, p.24.

issues marginalised and fed up of having to deal with women's rights as separate and distinct from human rights. Were women not human after all?

In the same year, Navi Pillay and Jessica Neuwirth established Equality Now which strives for the protection and promotion of the human rights of women around the world.

Human Rights of Women

In 1985, when Navi returned to South Africa after her sojourn in the USA, her attentions were drawn to another area of human rights which required immediate and drastic action: violence against and abuse of women in a society already fractured by racial hatred, brutality and stark injustices. In this dysfunctional society, the black woman was at the bottom of the pile, a victim of racial, gender, economic and cultural discrimination. Navi, from her experience as an attorney in the communities in and around Durban, knew that there were no shelters for abused women, and that the law did not allow for court orders which put an end to the domestic violence or removed the abusive husband from the matrimonial home. She stressed, at this point, in her writing on the subject and in interviews that it is the legal system which is to blame for discrimination and abuse of women. Bouvard has noted that Navi saw the denial of women's rights as 'grounded in the origins of South African law, English common law, Roman Dutch law, African customary law, Indian social systems, and Bantu law, all of which regard women as legal minors under the authority of a husband or guardian.'*

Once more, Navi was preparing for battle against the South African justice system but this time her strategy was different – she was going to directly empower women by translating what legal rights they did have into reality.

In 1986, Navi founded the Advice Desk for Abused Women together with friend and colleague Dr Anshu Padayachee. In an interview Dr Padayachee, a criminologist, described Navi and herself as 'mothers-in-arms'. To begin with, Navi and Anshu were mothers whose daughters were in primary school together (they are also distantly related) but after discovering their shared concerns they decided to take a stand by providing referral and support services for abused women. The Advice Desk was started in their homes with both women taking calls day and night. Social workers, welfare bodies and lawyers were coerced into volunteering their services. The main task of the Advice Desk was to instruct women on their legal

---

* MG Bouvard, p.256.

rights. The rudimentary Advice Desk began as a community organisation and then became a national network, later being bolstered by the support of Lawyers for Human Rights, a non-government organisation in South Africa. In addition to offering advice to women and setting up shelters, the Advice Desk has also made enormous efforts to garner media attention. Keeping the violation of women's rights in the media spotlight was another one of the strategies employed in this particular battle. Not one to squander valuable experience, and with her characteristic long-term vision, Navi co-authored a useful guide, *Violence Against Women: Rights and Remedies*, which served as an addendum to the *Family Violence Act* of 1993.

The Advice Desk (now called Advice Desk for the Abused so as to include *all* victims of domestic abuse) still exists and is housed on the campus of the University of KwaZulu-Natal where a group of dedicated men and women continue the work Navi began in the 1980s. The Desk has expanded its mission to foster social change through collaboration with community and grassroots organisations. Navi still helps by connecting the Advice Desk to her impressive international network of human rights organisations, and by advising Dr Padayachee who continues to train volunteers. Dr Padayachee's face lights up when Navi's name is mentioned and she describes her as 'an original thinker', someone with 'daredevil tenacity'.

Navi Pillay is one of those rare individuals who can juggle balls of varying sizes and hues. Whether it is answering the telephone call of a domestic abuse victim in her home or chairing a meeting in New York, Navi discharges her duties with dignity and dedication. After proclaiming a shift in her battle strategy in the early 1980s (Navi made it all too clear that there could not be political freedom in South Africa without the empowerment of women), Navi went on to tackle issues of women's rights internationally. With offices in New York, Nairobi and London, Equality Now works with national human rights organisations and individual activists across the world. Their mandate is to document violence and discrimination against women and mobilise international action to support their efforts to stop these human rights abuses. It has a Women's Action Network which coordinates efforts around the globe. Navi Pillay has retained her association with Equality Now but these days her interventions in women's rights are orchestrated from her desk in the Palais Wilson, Geneva, where she is based as United Nations High Commissioner for Human Rights. In her opinion piece issued on International Women's Day 2009, she reiterated her zeal for the issue of women's rights: 'As UN High Commissioner for Human Rights, my mandate is the protection and promotion of human rights, including women's rights for all women. I am concerned that the global economic crisis we are currently facing will have a disproportionate impact on women. Women are the majority of the poor and disenfranchised. Women face deprivation of economic and social rights, as well as civil and political rights. The recognition of all these rights, to which women are entitled, is fundamental to the empowerment of women.'

A cynical reader may perceive this extract as mere rhetoric, the claptrap of one in power who is accustomed to pandering to the world's media, but Navi Pillay is imbued with both clarity of purpose and the ability to articulate her vision. In 1996 when Navi realised that the women of South Africa could not be empowered through the courts alone, she co-founded a broad-based women's investment company, Nozala. She now serves the Nozala Trust which specifically addresses immediate economic needs through supporting business start-ups. Nozala's philosophy is to support equity investments with operational involvement and value-adding activities. For her efforts, the Women's Bureau of South Africa awarded Navi a certificate of merit for outstanding service to the South African community in November 1993.

The Dawn of a New Era

As Navi Pillay began moving in ever bigger, more powerful circles, her vision has remained steadfast. The sentiments in her International Women's Day speech echo ones expressed by the Women's National Coalition which was set up in South Africa in 1992 to help draft the fledgling democracy's new constitution. South Africa was poised on the brink of a bright new epoch: Nelson Mandela had been released from prison on 11 February 1990, plans were afoot for the country's first democratic elections in 1994, the ANC was grooming itself to become the government's ruling party, and the laws of the land were about to change for the greater good of each and every one of its citizens. Since her return from the USA, Navi's personal professional status had begun to gradually alter, reflecting the seismic shift of power which was beginning to occur on a national level. A year after completing her doctorate, in 1989, Navi began lecturing at the Department of Public Law at the University of Natal, the very institution which attempted to deny her the right to study for an LL.B. How the tide had changed!

Navi joined the legal working group at the national level of the Women's National Coalition which was comprised of about 108 regional bodies and organisations. This work, the drafting of a women's rights

charter, was grist to Navi's mill which had been grind-
ing away at the South African legal system for almost
two decades by this point. After much debate and
some dissension, the Coalition decided to push for
the inclusion in the constitution of an equality clause
which prohibited discrimination on the grounds of
gender, race, religion and sexual orientation. The
constitution of South Africa, widely regarded as one
of the most progressive in the world, also includes
a special statute which fundamentally changes the
status of women in the eyes of the law. Navi's pride
when describing this statute is hard to disguise: 'We
also have a special statute for the very first time on
the prevention of family violence, a statute which
removes discriminatory clauses against women in
about thirteen laws, guaranteeing that both parents
are now equal guardians and that the father is no
longer the head of the family. The same marriage
laws now apply to all race groups ...'*

Navi Pillay, the woman who white law firms would
not hire, the woman who was deemed a danger to
the state, and the woman who persevered against
the odds, had helped to re-write the laws of the land.
New laws and a new constitution meant that the land
which had run red with the blood of its sons and
daughters was being transformed into a democracy.

---

* MG Bouvard, p.262.

Navi's ability to multitask is astounding, and her contribution to the transformation process was appreciated in every sphere, it seems. Always a scholarly personality, Navi had been bitten by the academic bug whilst at Harvard. On her return to South Africa Navi shared the knowledge she had gleaned by lecturing and by serving as a member of the Law Faculty Board at the University of Durban-Westville. In 1992, Vinodh Jaichand, then the Dean of the Faculty of Law at the University of Durban-Westville, was responsible for making key institutional changes at the historically black university, which were in keeping with the new dispensation of the country: 'The composition of only white, male professors (who numbered no more than three at that time) and white members of the legal profession was changed to include new members who were representative of our society, including Navi Pillay and Justice Poswa.'*

Navi's contribution to academia and specifically to this Board was greatly appreciated and it was not long before she was appointed to the highest governing body of the university, the Council. This was achieved before her first term of office at the Faculty of Law Board ended.

As part of ongoing rehabilitation of South Africa's damaged society, the University of Durban-Westville

---

* Vinodh, Jaichand, [publication pending].

was later merged with the University of Natal to form the University of KwaZulu-Natal. The Vice-Principle of the University of Durban-Westville at the time, 2003, was Saths Cooper, a political activist and former Robben Island inmate, who was known and respected by Navi. In an interview Navi admitted that one of her greatest regrets is that she was not more outspoken during her early years as a lawyer, proffering Saths Cooper and Strini Moodley as two of a new breed of freedom fighters whose cavalier form of defiance impressed her and taught her a new temerity. Although, looking back on her life from an external perspective, one can not accuse Navi of reticence or cowardice.

Now, Navi Pillay, once relegated to a warehouse in the section of campus designated for black students, was on the Council of the university. Her husband, Gaby, was also employed at the university as the head of the Legal Aid Clinic at the Centre for Human Rights and Community Law. Although Gaby and Navi's lives had taken divergent paths for many years (by the early 1990s their marriage was pretty much on the rocks) they still shared some fundamental beliefs and interests. In addition to his post at the Legal Aid Clinic, over the years Gaby had served as the treasurer of the Black Lawyers' Association, and as an executive member of the New Unity Movement. In very different capacities they both served the common goal of achieving human rights for their fellow citizens.

Enter Judge Navi Pillay

Navi's skills, enthusiasm, and energy know no bounds and many South African institutions, such as Lawyers for Human Rights for which she served as a trustee on their board, or Nozala, have benefited from her knowledge and expertise. When the first democratic elections were held in South Africa in 1994, and Nelson Mandela, the world's most famous political prisoner, became the country's president, it was time for a shakedown of the judiciary. The country was ready for its first black female Supreme Court judge. Minister of Justice, Mr Dullah Omar, personally telephoned Navi at home and asked her if she was up to the challenge of serving as an acting judge in the Natal Provincial Division of the Supreme Court. On 31 January 1995, Judge Pillay entered the chambers of a judge in a South African court for the first time, and they were her own chambers! Even more sensational, the counsel was to address her as 'My Lord, Your Lordship', according to the British model of courtroom etiquette.

Although Navi was exhausted, having been embroiled for months in a very high-profile murder case which set a controversial precedent, she was ebullient about her new post. In the case State vs Xerxes Nursingh, 1994, Navi had examined the relevance of child sexual abuse to the defence of sane automatism in parricide cases. Always thorough and calling on her international connections, she had worked in collaboration with expert psychiatrists from the USA and the California appellate project. Using this argument of sane automatism or temporary insanity, Navi Pillay was able to successfully defend Xerxes Nursingh who had murdered his mother and grandparents. One of her first cases on the bench was also harrowing and saw her sentencing a rapist to twenty years' imprisonment. In an interview with a reporter at the time, Navi was candid about the emotional strain she was under: 'The responsibilities weigh heavily on my mind and I often lie awake at night pondering the facts that have been brought before me.'*

But the role of Supreme Court judge was not the only thing weighing heavily on Navi's mind. 1995 was also the year that Navi and Gaby were divorced. By this time Gaby was dependent on alcohol and ill. He brought a lawsuit against Navi over the jointly owned family home and his right to reside there. The media, hungry for a scandal, exploited the irony that a high

* John Nichols, 'She's Called "My Lord,"' *The Natal Witness*, 28 February 1995.

profile human rights lawyer was being accused of violating her ex-husband's right to their jointly owned property. Never one to squander a legal opportunity, Navi lodged a counter claim. Once more Navi was in full battle mode but this time the cause was personal. She was defiant and her claims of excessive drinking and abuse no doubt severely damaged Gaby's case. After years of advising women about their rights in the domestic sphere, she was defending her own home and her two children. Although the outcome of this painful dispute was never clear, Navi has remained loyal to the memory of Gaby who died a few years later in the disputed family home in Durban. Gaby's obituary in local papers was headed 'Human rights lawyer dies'.

For Navi it was the end of an era. She had reached the pinnacle of her career within the national boundaries of South Africa. She had achieved many of her goals but there was perhaps some disappointment that she had not been appointed to the Constitutional Court of South Africa. In 1994, she applied for the position of judge on the Constitutional Court and was subjected to a gruelling interview by the Judicial Service Commission but her application was not successful. One theory about this failed application is that Navi's concern about a 'right to life' article in the South African constitution, a concern which she raised in her interview, may have marred her prospects. Navi stated her case explicitly and defi-antly: the article could potentially raise problems for women seeking an abortion; the pro-life lobby could latch onto this clause; the article was not clear on defining the right to life and when the right began; and the blurriness of the wording could be used against women's reproductive rights. Despite the set-back Navi stuck to her guns, and in a later chapter of her life she was to become known as the 'abortion advocate' in the US press.

Another blow at this stage was that her marriage had ended in a cloud of public scandal, and it was per-haps serendipitous that greater challenges beckoned on the world stage. When the United Nations set up the International Criminal Tribunal in Rwanda, Navi was an obvious candidate for the position of judge. Of the twelve candidates selected, Navi was the only one who received fifteen unanimous votes from the United Nations Security Council. This was yet again a milestone – Navi Pillay was the first South African judge to be appointed to serve in this capacity in an international court. Towards the end of 1995, Navi left South Africa for Tanzania to begin a new, even more challenging and trail-blazing chapter in her remarkable life.

World Justice

Everyone is entitled in full equality to a fair and
public hearing by an independent and impartial
tribunal, in the determination of his rights and
obligations and of any criminal charge against him.
(Article 10. Universal Declaration of Human Rights)

Serving An International Tribunal

Arusha is a town halfway between Cape and Cairo
in the north-east of Tanzania. It nestles in the foot-
hills of Mount Meru close to famous areas of exceptional natural beauty such as the Serengeti National
Park, Arusha National Park, Mount Kilimanjaro, the
Great Rift Valley and the Ngorongoro Crater. The
town is surrounded by rose plantations and coffee
estates and boasts some of the most fertile fruit and
vegetable plantations in Africa. Arusha is also where
the headquarters of the United Nations International

Criminal Tribunal for Rwanda (ICTR) is situated. The sleepy, picturesque town has played host to some of the world's most high-profile human rights lawyers, to some of the world's most monstrous human rights violators, and to some of the most pitiable victims of human rights violations that the world has seen. After shuttling between Durban and Arusha for a while, Navi Pillay made Arusha her home in 1996. She had been appointed as a judge on the ICTR.

When Navi arrived in Arusha she claims she was shocked. The infrastructure of the town was poor. The unreliable electricity supply, unpurified water, and the badly maintained roads gave her a few misgivings. She recalls with good humour that on two occasions she had to help push her vehicle out of the mud when it became bogged down en route to the courthouse. But the indomitable Navi shrugged off these personal discomforts as being 'all in a day's work'. She soon worked out a survival strategy – she carried precious spices and other foodstuffs with her from South Africa, and she made the most of the rich Tanzanian soil by planting the herbs she needed to cook her beloved Indian curries. Then she had to contend with the exigencies of her job. Before being assigned an apartment she worked in hotel rooms, and there were times when she read documents at night by candlelight. The windows of her apartment were sealed for security reasons but the ever-optimistic Navi

pointed out that from her office she had a hearten-
ing view of Mount Kilimanjaro. Also, a UN security
guard escorted her everywhere she went. The security
guard, who was female, seemed to send out a signal
to the inhabitants of Arusha and to the international
media that had turned its spotlight on the ICTR –
here was a tough woman intent on getting the job
done and who believed in the equality of the sexes.
For Navi these were necessary adjustments. She had
to adjust quickly to living away from her family and
friends in fairly primitive and isolated conditions, so
that she could turn her attention to the serious task of
serving the ICTR as a Trial Chamber judge.

Yet the wrench from her daughters, now university
students, had been painful. In 1995, Isvari was completing a Bachelor of Arts degree at the University
of Durban-Westville, and Kamini had just begun a
degree in town planning at the University of Natal,
her mother's *alma mater*. The girls were left to run
the family home in Durban which was home also
to their increasingly frail grandfather, Narrainsamy,
and their alcohol-dependent father, Gaby. They were
very fortunate to have Beatrice Hlope as a live-in
housekeeper, but the responsibilities heaped on their
young shoulders were heavy. In an interview, Kamini
repudiated any notion that she and Isvari felt resent-
ment towards their mother for shifting this load onto
them. On the contrary, Kamini and Isvari seem to

view the experience in a positive light. The sisters banded together to cope with their adult responsibilities, and more significantly to them, their mother had a once-in-a-lifetime opportunity to make a huge, positive impact on the world. Instead of reflecting badly on Navi as a mother, what this situation reveals is that Isvari and Kamini have inherited their mother's selflessness and sense of perspective – the ability to weigh up one's own needs against the needs of others and to act in favour of that which is greater. For Navi and her daughters the needs of the people of Rwanda won hands down.

The Security Council of the United Nations created the ICTR by Resolution 955 of 8 November 1994 in order to address the serious violations of humanitarian law which were committed in Rwanda between 1 January 1994 and 31 December 1994. The ICTR is governed by its statute which is annexed to Resolution 955, and the Rules of Procedure and Evidence which the judges adopted is in accordance with this statute. These Rules of Procedure and Evidence provide the framework for the judicial system. The ICTR consists of three organs: the Chambers and the Appeals Chamber (the organ Navi Pillay served directly); the Office of the Prosecutor, which is in charge of investigations and prosecutions; and the Registry, which provides overall judicial and administrative support to the Chambers and the Prosecutor.

The ICTR is vested with the power to prosecute persons who commit humanitarian crimes as part of a widespread or systematic attack against any civilian population on national, political, ethnic, racial or religious grounds. These humanitarian crimes are listed as: murder, extermination, enslavement, deportation, imprisonment, torture, rape, persecutions and other inhumane acts. During the period stipulated by the ICTR, and in particular between the months of April and July 1994, approximately 800,000 Rwandans were killed, in what many consider to be a campaign of extermination directed against Tutsis and moderate Hutus. Some fifteen years later the ICTR is still active, still prosecuting crimes from that heinous period.

An Impartial Judge

Navi Pillay was appointed as judge to Trial Chamber I of the Chambers and Appeals Chamber. To begin with, she was the only female judge at the ICTR and she worked alongside Judge Laïty Kama of Senegal, Judge Yakov Ostrovsky of Russia, and Judge Lennart Aspegren of Sweden. In this role of judge, clad in the judicial garb of stiff collar and red and black gown, her main tasks were to listen to the testimony of those being prosecuted, and of the victims of genocide, and then to question them. To uphold the lofty principles of justice impartiality was imperative, but Navi's compassion was stirred. In addition to the court testimonies, she also watched video footage and slides, and visited the sites of massacres. But it was the testimony of witnesses, those who had lived through hell and survived the worst brutalities, those who came to tell their chilling stories, those who sought justice, that most moved Navi. Further, because the ICTR's statute is based on common law rather than civil law, which permits reliable hearsay from witnesses, witness testimonies were crucial for the functioning of the ICTR. Over the years since its inception, the ICTR has pioneered advocacy for victim-oriented restitutive justice in international criminal law. This concept has now been included in the statute of the International Criminal Court.

In an interview shortly after leaving the ICTR, Navi explained her reaction to these testimonies: 'I will carry with me for the rest of my life the accounts of suffering and atrocity told by survivors. Each day I would think I had heard the worst ... Survivors told how they hid under bodies for days and pretended to be dead ... We [judges] would fall asleep with exhaustion and wake up in the morning and relive the testimonies ... It has taught me to stop complaining.'

Navi's concern for the victims was apparent. Most crucially though, Navi Pillay had to learn to put aside any emotional response she may have had to these testimonies in order to fulfil her role as impartial judge in a court of law. In what must be singular effort and resolve, Navi managed to retain her empathy as a human being, whilst when she donned the judicial garb of a judge, she served only one purpose – the supreme principle of justice. In the court she became detached, measured in her tone, her face assuming a deadpan expression. For Navi, her focus was clear. She was there to rout out 'individual criminal responsibility' and to 'judge each case on evidence presented in the courtroom'. Those who have had the privilege to see Judge Navi Pillay at work at the ICTR have commented on her dignified demeanour, her calm confidence, and professionalism. Those same people have been struck also by her care and concern for the victims of Rwanda's genocide.

Fifteen years after assuming the role of judge at the ICTR, Navi Pillay, UN High Commissioner for Human Rights saluted those witnesses she had listened to in Arusha. On 1 April 2009, in an address to commemorate the fifteenth anniversary of the genocide in Rwanda, Navi Pillay referred to these witnesses as 'heroes' whose brave actions made justice possible:

This is also an opportunity to pay homage to the witnesses who came forward with harrowing accounts of atrocities. These individuals refused to remain silent and tacitly tolerant about violations of human rights. Their testimony helped to dismantle barriers to dialogue and to mend and restore the very foundations of peaceful coexistence, for it is the establishment of truth that fosters reconciliation.

In expressing their grief and horror, survivors in Rwanda did not choose the barren path of wanton revenge, but that of justice and thereby cleared the way for communal rebuilding. They sought the help of the international community to bolster their efforts. These are the heroes whose courage gives life to the rule of law as a standard of human conduct in the world.*

In these two paragraphs a clear vision is discernible in Navi Pillay's rhetoric, a vision which was first glimpsed in the essays of a schoolgirl: every human being on this planet deserves justice and it is every human being's responsibility to help achieve and maintain justice. For Navi, achieving a symbiosis between the victims of genocide and an international judicial system is the goal that gave her the strength to be an impartial judge in the ICTR.

---

* For transcripts of speeches see OHCHR official website http:// www.ohchr.org/EN/Pages/WelcomePage.aspx

Battles Won

The ICTR had a lot riding on its shoulders, however ad hoc it was to begin with and notwithstanding the enormity of its proposed undertaking. In many ways the ICTR was attempting to break new ground in international criminal law, and thus the international legal fraternity and other stakeholders held their breaths while the fledgling court tested its wings. The ICTR did not disappoint. It was the first international tribunal to try the crime of genocide, and it was the first international tribunal to try a head of government for international crimes, including genocide and other crimes against humanity. Former Rwandan Prime Minister, Jean Kambanda, was indicted, convicted of crimes against humanity, and sentenced to life imprisonment. Navi Pillay sat on the bench that tried Kambanda.

The ICTR was also the first known court, international or municipal, to hold that sexual violence can be an act of genocide. Judge Navi Pillay sat on the bench which presided over this landmark case. On 30 May 1996 the former *bourgmestre* of Taba, a commune in Rwanda, Mr Jean-Paul Akayesu, was brought before Trial Chamber I. Fifteen charges of genocide, crimes against humanity, and violations of

Article 3 common to the Geneva Conventions* were brought against him. He pleaded not guilty to all the charges. During the trial several of the victim-witnesses recounted acts of sexual violence perpetrated against them. But Akayesu was not being charged with sexual violence offences. Faced with this conundrum, Navi Pillay posed a question to the Office of the Prosecutor: what are the judges expected to do with the evidence of sexual violence in a trial where there are no charges relating to sexual violence and the main charge is genocide?

As a direct result of Navi Pillay's pointed question, the Prosecution filed an indictment which later led to the finding that rape may under certain circumstances constitute genocide. Chile Eboe-Osuji, who worked in the Office of the Prosecutor at the time and who is now the ICTR's Head of Chambers, sums up the significance of the Akayesu trial: 'The striking value of Akayesu's conclusion – that sexual violence can be an act of genocide – lies in the fact that none of the leading instruments of international criminal law, which are the primary sources of the law of genocide, mention sexual violence specifically as an act of genocide. However, the reasoning that sexual violence can be an act of genocide has not agitated much disagreement. The general acceptance of the reasoning is not explained

---

* See Glossary of Terms

by considerations of political correctness, but by the deductive reasoning unassailably deployed by Judge Pillay and her two colleagues in the Akayesu case.'*

Chile Eboe-Osuji goes on to explain the impact this trial has had on international criminal law: 'This provision has now been incorporated directly and repeatedly into the leading modern instruments on the subject of international criminal law, such as the Statutes of the International Criminal Tribunal for Rwanda, the International Criminal Tribunal for the former Yugoslavia and the International Criminal Court.'† After the landmark verdict was given, Navi was jubilant about the achievement yet concerned that the verdict should act as a deterrent in the future. In a general statement to the press she declared, 'From time immemorial, rape has been regarded as spoils of war. Now it will be considered a war crime. We want to send out a strong signal that rape is no longer a trophy of war.'

In the same year that the Akayesu trial began, Navi received an unexpected accolade. Together with the South African Speaker of the House of Parliament, Dr Frene Ginwala, Navi was nominated for the position of United Nations Secretary-General.

---

* Chile Eboe-Osuji, 'Navi Pillay in Her Age: An Introduction', [publication pending].
† Chile Eboe-Osuji, [publication pending].

According to press coverage at the time, Navi's nomination was endorsed by women's rights organisations around the world. Not only was the nomination an honour for Navi, the fact that two South African women had been nominated was a coup for the country. Although South Africans came out in full support of the nominees, even submitting a petition to President Mandela, Frene Ginwala and Navi Pillay both lost out to Ghanaian diplomat, Kofi Annan.

A few years later, in May 1999, Navi received the well-deserved and apt recognition of being appointed as President of the ICTR for a four-year term. Her appointment was met with much delight from supporters around the world (who sent 500 roses to her apartment in Arusha) and from high-ranking officials (UN Secretary-General Kofi Annan and US Secretary of State Madeleine Albright both sent her warm letters of congratulations). Later in the same year she received a Noel Foundation/United Nations Development Fund for Women (UNIFEM) Award for Compassion. The ICTR was expanding – the number of judges had increased to nine, which led to the establishment of a third Trial Chamber. While serving as President of the ICTR, Navi was also Presiding Judge of Trial Chamber I. This means that although her administrative responsibilities increased enormously (as President of the ICTR,

Navi had to prepare and present annual reports to the United Nations General Assembly and Security Council), she maintained her high level of trial activity. Not one to squander an opportunity for reform, Navi took important statutory initiatives whilst President of the ICTR. These initiatives were aimed at bringing the ICTR up to par with the International Criminal Tribunal for the former Yugoslavia (ICTY) which had been formed in 1991 and was based in The Hague. Moreover, Navi sought to increase the efficiency of the ICTR by acquiring more judges and by improving communication between the Registry and Chambers. From the accounts and anecdotes of former colleagues it seems that Navi prioritised judicial efficiency, addressing backlogs and bottlenecks. Her administrative reforms, although serving the common purpose – justice – were not always welcomed by colleagues but indisputably increased productivity at the ICTR.

On 3 December 2003 Navi delivered her final judgment at the ICTR. Never fearful of courting controversy, she found three media bosses guilty of inciting hate. The 'media case' as it was dubbed, led to a 361-page judgment of historic importance. During the 238 days in the courtroom, the hazy borderline between freedom of expression and the prohibition of incitement to genocide was debated. This was a mammoth case to preside over, and Navi had the added challenge of powerful, influential personalities in the courtroom. One of the accused even boycotted the trial. Former colleague and ICTR judge, Erik Møse, describes Navi's handling of yet another landmark ICTR case: 'But Navi presided with fairness, efficiency, authority and style, as in her other cases as presiding judge. It was a pleasure to form part of her Bench.'*

This case too was a first, breaking new legal ground by recognising the causal link between the ethnic hatred propagated by the media in Rwanda and the violence that took place in 1994. Navi, it would appear, never sacrificed impartiality or dignity in the court, and never shied away from pronouncing controversial verdicts, whatever the conditions.

The overall achievement of the ICTR to date is stupendous. Individuals have been indicted and extradited, victims have been given the opportunity to tell their stories and receive justice, precedents in international criminal justice have been laid down, a complex judicial institution has been set up in Arusha and Kigali, and the cooperation of the international community in maintaining justice has been achieved.

---

* Erik Møse, 'On the Bench with Navi' in Chile Eboe-Osuji (ed.), *Protecting Humanity in the Age of Navi: Essays* [publication pending].

However, the ICTR has its detractors and one of the first criticisms levelled at it was the amount of time it took for the wheel of justice to turn in Arusha. It took two years after setting up the ICTR before the first trial got underway. Navi was questioned about this in numerous interviews and her rebuttal was concise and practical: 'In a fair trial, the judicial process is slow.'* As Judge President of the ICTR Navi had to contest the view that the ICTR had not performed to its optimum capacity. She did this in her inimitable, no-nonsense manner, explaining: how long it took to coordinate judges from around the world and to agree on the rules of procedure; that it took a while to renovate and build the courts and detention centres in Arusha; that the prosecutor† had to investigate cases before bringing indictments against suspects; and that suspects had to be extradited from other countries. Judge Erik Møse of the ICTR substantiates this explanation with his memories of the founding of the ICTR: 'It is easy to forget how difficult the situation was in the early days of the Tribunal. Building a new institution is always a challenge, and the ICTR was no exception. As late as November

---

* Charmaine Pillay, 'Judging Genocide', *The Natal Post*, 25 June 1997, p.3.
† The prosecutor at this time was Judge Louise Arbour of Canada, whom Navi Pillay later succeeded as UN High Commissioner for Human Rights.

1995, there were no courtrooms, prisons, offices, legal officers or secretaries. There were no computers and no books. The judges had one telephone, placed in President Kama's office. Until September 1996, the judges shuttled between their home countries and Arusha, where they reviewed indictments for confirmation, issued warrants of arrest, etc.'*

Perhaps more pointed a criticism was that by March 2006 the ICTR had tried only officials of the former Hutu-led interim government of Rwanda, suggesting that other ethnic groups were not involved in the perpetration of atrocities in 1994. Navi was unequivocal in her refutation of this claim: '[O]ur statute mandates us to try people who are suspected to have committed serious offences in Rwanda in 1994 ... It does not target one ethnic group. ... It is the prosecutor who determines who should be investigated and indicted ... she bases her decisions on the evidence available.'†

As President of the ICTR, Navi was forced into the hazardous realm of public relations. To keep her focus clear, she never strayed far from the rule of the law. This was to be her mainstay and her consistent recourse again and again when the ship of justice hit stormy waters – as long as Navi was confident that

---

* Erik Møse, [publication pending].

† Alfred Ngotezi, 'We Neither Target Nor Favour Any Groups in Rwanda', *The East African*, 20 March 2000, p.26.

justice was being served, she was willing to face the detractors. She was adamant that the ICTR was operating in good faith and that both Hutus and Tutsis, as well as any other ethnic group, in Rwanda were receiving justice.

The Situation in South Africa

When Navi left her home country to take up her post at the ICTR, a similar body was being formed in South Africa. The Truth and Reconciliation Commission (TRC) was formed in accordance with the *Promotion of National Unity and Reconciliation Act*, No. 34 of 1995. The TRC was not a court of justice like the ICTR and the mandate was not to prosecute the villains of apartheid, but rather to give victims the opportunity to recount their stories of violations, and to give perpetrators the opportunity to confess their crimes and appeal for amnesty.

Unlike the ICTR which was governed by the principles of justice, the TRC acquired its rationale from the discipline of psychology. Collective memories, shared narratives, catharsis, conciliation, healing and recovery were some of the notions that informed the TRC. At its head sat the Chairperson, Bishop Desmond Tutu, who often broke down and openly wept whilst listening to testimonies. What the two bodies have in common is that they both seek truth and they both strive to restore dignity to the human beings who have been robbed of their human rights. When the TRC presented its report on 28 October 1998 it found that both the former apartheid government and elements of the liberation forces were guilty of human rights violations.

Despite its noble aims and impartial verdict, in South Africa it is still hotly debated as to whether the TRC has had any lasting value for a society which is today plagued by divisions, violence and poverty. Perhaps a United Nations ad hoc tribunal such as the ICTR would have served South Africa better. Speaking to an ICTR reporter on the eve of her inauguration as a judge in the International Criminal Court in The Hague in 2003, Navi revealed her disappointment that South Africa was never granted a judicial mechanism such as the ICTR: 'Apartheid, for instance, was declared a crime against humanity, but no mechanism was set up to prosecute such a crime. Very many people in positions of authority who perpetrated crimes of apartheid have escaped prosecution …'

For a judicial bloodhound like Navi, the idea that the perpetrators of apartheid were being granted impunity was anathema to what she had struggled for all her life – the tenacious sniffing out and legal articulation of the truth so that justice could be served. But South Africa's continuing bumpy ride towards peace and stability was not the only thing causing Navi heartache. When she left for Arusha in 1995 she had been embroiled in a legal battle with ex-husband, Gaby. Now four years on he was dead, but the circumstances of his death remain murky. His attorney issued a statement stating that Gaby had fallen, hit his head and died. Navi, understandably, did not share her feelings with the media at this time, but sister Jenny recalls that a private plane was chartered to fly Navi home so that she could attend Gaby's funeral. Navi and Gaby had started a life together full of hope and promise in a land that would deny them not only their dreams but their fundamental human rights. Somehow they triumphed over the many obstacles their external world, and even biology, had strewn in their path. Sadly, in their most private world, they were not able to transcend the barriers which stood between them.

However, 1999 was to end joyously for Navi because her elder daughter's colourful Hindu wedding took place in December of that year. Isvari married Jayandren Pather and together they moved to New York, a city much visited by Navi who has many friends and comrades there. It is fortunate that Navi travels to New York frequently for work because in 2007 she became the proud grandmother of Sendhil, a young boy who has yet to learn about his grandmother's illustrious life.

Moving On

In December 2003, after the delivery of the 'media case' judgment, Navi left the ICTR and Arusha to take up a position as judge at the International Criminal Court at The Hague. Her former colleagues in Arusha remember her with awe, respect, and surprisingly, with mischievous humour. An assistant describes her as 'the tornado', referring to the commanding manner she used to issue instructions the moment she stepped foot in the office. Others recall that she 'bribed them with biscuits' after a bout of tetchiness, and that her generosity was democratic, distributing chocolate, home-made cakes and snacks to the secretaries of the Chamber. In particular, one former secretary recalls without rancour how Navi Pillay's zeal and determination forced her to sometimes be 'quick and sharp' with colleagues – surely this is a polite way of saying she did not suffer fools gladly! Navi immersed herself in the world of the ICTR and that included the parties and various social functions she was invited to. Her colleagues and staff caught a glimpse of the woman inside the judge's gown when she took a whole contingent of them to South Africa for her birthday – 'She was so hospitable to us that we all had to pinch one another in surprise!' exclaims the young woman. The same woman then jokingly threatens to visit Navi in

Europe, hoping for more of the same warmth and hospitality from her host.

The International Criminal Court

On 11 March 2003 the International Criminal Court (ICC) was inaugurated at The Hague. Although the ICC is the first independent, international, treaty-based criminal court the world has seen, there have been a few precursors and much multilateral planning for such an organisation. Shortly after World War Two the Nuremberg and Tokyo trials were set up to address war crimes, crimes against peace, and crimes against humanity committed during the war. In the 1990s tribunals such as the ICTR and the ICTY were set up to deal with crimes committed within the context of specific conflicts. Through the processes and experiences of these international trials and tribunals, the international legal community was able to reach a consensus on definitions of genocide, crimes against humanity and war crimes, although, of course, these definitions are evolving every day as trailblazers like Navi Pillay extend the frontiers of justice.

The dialogue and judicial process which preceded the formation of the ICC were complex and protracted. A key date is 17 July 1998 when 120 states adopted the Rome Statute. This Statute is the legislation, in this case an international treaty, on which the ICC is based. The states which formally express their consent to be bound by the provisions of the Rome Statute are known as 'parties', and in July 2009, 110 states were recorded 'parties'. Literature disseminated by the ICC emphasises that it is independent and not part of the United Nations, although the two organisations often work in tandem. The ICC will only intervene when the most serious contraventions of international criminal law have been committed, and it is only called into action as a last resort. In the first instance, national judicial systems are encouraged to try criminals of this calibre and to not grant them impunity. The ICC is constituted of four organs: the Presidency; the Judicial Divisions; the Office of the Prosecutor; and the Registry.

In February 2003 an assembly of the 'parties' of the Rome Statute elected the first eighteen judges to the Judicial Divisions which are comprised of the Pre-Trial Division, the Trial Division and the Appeals Division. Navi Pillay, who had proven her mettle as a judge and an administrator at the ICTR was elected as a judge in the Appeals Division of the ICC. But these were not propitious times for the principle of international judicial cooperation. A month later in March 2003, President George W. Bush launched the USA (and its allies) into a war against Iraq. This was a unilateral decision which flouted the resolution of the UN Security Council. To make matters worse, the USA refused to ratify the Rome Statute, thus alienating itself from the ICC and the notion of international criminal justice. In September 2004, UN Secretary-General Kofi Annan went so far as to declare that the war in Iraq was illegal because it contravened the UN Charter. These were indeed trying times for those who dreamed of world justice, and as Navi Pillay began her six-year term at the ICC, she had to dig deep to remain steadfast in her belief that the ICC could operate as a deterrent to those who would disavow the human rights of others.

Navi was the only female judge in the Appeals Division, which is composed of the President of the Court, and four other judges. When asked if she encountered gender discrimination in the workplace Navi's response is brief yet telling: 'They are forced to treat me as a professional.' For a stalwart campaigner against discrimination like Navi, the strategy for survival in a male-dominated workplace was simply excellence. Her job demanded excellence and that is what she delivered, thus insulating her from the barbs of prejudice. The Appeals Division has assigned to it an Appeals Chamber composed of the five judges of the Division. The Appeals Chamber is the highest tier in the judiciary and is thus the final arbiter on legal issues arising in the course of pre-trial and trial proceedings. Being involved in this highest level of arbitration was not Navi's only job. She also served as President of the Court of the Appeals Division for a year. In this capacity Navi had to juggle her judicial tasks with administrative issues arising within the Division.

True to form, Navi left her mark on the ICC when, as presiding judge, she drafted the judgment in the first appeal of the Court. The judgment pertained to the prosecutor's application for warrants of arrest, and it has lasting impact because it inter alia underscored the fact that the ICC's jurisdiction extends not only to the most notorious perpetrators of human rights violations but to all those responsible for criminal acts. Following this achievement, Navi presided over the very first appeals on victim participation in trial and pre-trial proceedings. In the 'Judgment on the Appeals of The Prosecutor and The Defence against Trial Chamber I's Decision on Victims' Participation of 18 January 2008', the Appeals Chamber recognised the right of victims to actively participate in the trial by leading evidence against the accused as well as, when deemed appropriate, questioning the accused. This was seen as a victory by human rights organisations as well as victims' representatives worldwide. Although Navi had been involved in championing the rights of victims to bear testimony in court at the ICTR, the Rome Statute had yet to recognise the concept of victim-oriented restitutive justice. Now, victims' participation in trials is a generally accepted element of international criminal proceedings.

Natasha Naidoo, a legal officer in the Appeals Division, who worked closely with Navi during her tenure, described an average day for Navi at the ICC: 'An average day would start around nine a.m. and end (depending on our deadlines) around six thirty p.m. Navi would often lunch in her office with me, enjoying delicious curry that she would have prepared that morning. ... Navi would often have various speaking engagements on top of her busy judicial workload. She was also part of many working groups within the judiciary which was tasked with putting in place procedures for proper management and long-term projects within the court.' Perhaps more remarkable than the gruelling schedule described here is the fact that Judge Navi Pillay prepared her own lunch every day, and then shared it with her colleagues!

On the subjects of working with Navi and her subsequent departure, her former colleagues at the ICC echo the sentiments of the ICTR staff. She is remembered with respect and admiration, and her reputation for being straightforward yet approachable is very much alive. The overwhelming sentiment though is one of pride – the staff at the ICC is proud that one of their own is now the UN High

Commissioner for Human Rights. Natasha Naidoo summed up this collegial pride (which in South Africa extends to national pride): 'To this day staff from all sectors of the ICC still ask after her and are quick to let me know that they saw her on the news or read about her bold human rights strides.'

The ICC, like the ICTR, took a while to get going. For years the activities of the ICC have been mainly investigative. In 2003, the prosecutor initiated investigations into war crimes and crimes against humanity in the Ituri region of the DRC. Then in 2005, five arrest warrants were issued for the senior officers in the Lord's Resistance Army (LRA) in Uganda but these suspects, bar one who is dead, are still at large. These indictments sparked a wave of criticism by those who saw the ICC as devaluing traditional judicial systems. Following on in 2007, the ICC began investigating crimes committed in the Central African Republic. But it was not until 26 January 2009 that the first trial began at The Hague. Currently on trial is Thomas Lubanga Dyilo, a former warlord from north-eastern Congo, who is charged with enlisting and conscripting children under the age of fifteen as soldiers and using them to participate actively in combat. Although Lubanga's forces are alleged to have committed various other crimes such as killing, rape and torture, the ICC has not charged him with these crimes.

Most of the investigations have progressed to the

pre-trial stage, but many of those accused still elude the long arm of the ICC, and those who desire justice have learned to be patient. Making headlines in recent times has been the arrest of Omar Hassan Ahmad al-Bashir, former President of the Republic of Sudan, who is charged with five counts of crimes against humanity and two counts of war crimes. Many critics have spoken out against Bashir's indictment, warning that this could endanger the people of Darfur who could be targeted by government-backed militia. Reprisals would scupper the work of humanitarian organisations and peacekeepers, plunging the region into further chaos and strife.

Arguably the main critic or opponent of the ICC has been the government of the USA. According to the Rome Statute, the UN Security Council is able to prompt action by the Court or to obstruct prosecutions. The USA, as one of the five permanent members of the Security Council, has used its power of veto to demonstrate objections to the Court. The main reason, it would appear, for this undermining of the ICC is that the USA wishes to ensure immunity of US nationals from prosecution by the Court. Despite criticism and opposition, be it of a judicial, political or practical nature, the work of the ICC continues, and people like Navi Pillay who believe that justice is a force for good, continue to debate, ponder, and adjudicate the most invidious of human crimes.

Just before taking up her position at the ICC, Navi was asked if she would return to South Africa when her term of office ended. She answered with typical good-humour and self-deprecation but with a distinct lack of prophecy: 'Yes, but I think I will be too old to work as a judge. My term here is six years and I am now sixty-two.'

During her six-year term at The Hague, Navi was to lose her father and mainstay, Narrainsamy Naidoo, who died at the age of 100. Shortly after his death she worked hard to trace his existing family in India. She managed to trace them to a small village called Vathalagundu, near Chennai in Tamil Nadu. In a characteristically generous gesture she took a group of family members with her to meet her new-found relatives. Navi's dedication to her family rivals her dedication to the cause of justice, so when she witnessed the poverty of her extended family in India, she decided to sponsor the education of some of the younger members. It takes a rare spirit and formidable ability for someone in Navi's position to spare the time to research her genealogy, to then reunite two branches of a family split by colonial forces, and to top it all with a gesture of great compassion and generosity. Her daughter Kamini says that Navi takes a great interest in the welfare of the younger generations in the family, and she appears to have led by example, inspiring many a wayward youth to find meaning and purpose in life by studying law. According to Kamini, there is a running joke in the family that Navi has managed to make everyone else lawyers except her daughters. Going on the evidence, her sway has extended beyond the family, for every now and again strangers will approach Navi and declare gushingly, 'I studied law because of you!'

On a more serious note, Kamini believes that, as a mother of such passion and conviction, Navi instilled in her a 'profound sense of duty towards her country'. According to Kamini, Navi does not care what your profession is as long as you make a contribution to society. It is probably for this reason that Kamini now works in the public sector. She is a Director of Development Planning and Urban Management for the Johannesburg City Council. Inspired by her mother to utilise her skills in public service, Kamini is involved in drawing up strategic plans for schools, roads and social facilities. Years earlier in 1995, when Kamini was at university, she showed she was her mother's daughter when she spoke out against corruption in KwaZulu-Natal's Ministry of Transport. When Kamini went to a testing ground to take a driving test, she was asked to pay a bribe to the inspector. When she refused to pay the bribe she was failed, but the feisty young woman did not slink away with her tail between her legs. She consulted with an expert legal brain, her mother, and went to the press with the story. Kamini was motivated by a concern for the growing levels of corruption in almost every sector of South African society. Although just nineteen years old, her conscience was troubled by the fact that as a consequence of the corruption, unfit drivers were putting lives at risk on the already hazardous South African roads. There can be no clearer testimony to Navi's power to effect good works than Kamini's sense of duty and these words uttered by her, 'I've learned from my mother to give back to my country.'

It is this combination of the highflying international public figure using reason and intellect to serve the whole of humanity, with the quiet empathy and consideration of the private individual, which forms the bedrock of Navi's unique personality – a personality most suited for the demanding and tricky role of United Nations High Commissioner for Human Rights.

Realising Human Rights For All

*Everyone is entitled to all the rights and freedoms
set forth in this Declaration, without distinction
of any kind, such as race, colour, sex, language,
religion, political or other opinion, national or
social origin, property, birth or other status.*
(Article 2. Universal Declaration of Human Rights)

A Personal Credo

On 21 February 2008 Navi Pillay presented the second
Annual Distinguished Lecture on Criminal Justice
and Human Rights at the Centre for Criminal Justice and Human Rights, University College Cork, Ire-
land. In this speech Navi articulated her conception
of international law: 'International law increasingly
plays a role in shaping state policy and domestic law
in advancing protection of human rights. If we add to
this trend, the growth of international criminal law

and its emphasis on the criminal responsibility of the individual, the picture is clear: the role of the individual as the subject and object of international law is unassailable.'*

Navi was poised at a cusp in her professional life when she made this speech. Almost at the end of her term of office at the International Criminal Court, and about to begin a new chapter as the UN High Commissioner for Human Rights, she was now aged sixty-seven with forty-three years of service as a legal practitioner. Navi, at this point, had ample experience and knowledge to shape a cogent credo on the subject which has always been closest to her heart – the relationship between law and human rights. The speech in Cork adumbrated this credo which informs and sustains her new high-pressure, high-profile position.

For Navi Pillay international law is an instrument par excellence which strives for and upholds human rights for all persons on the planet. She believes that through international mechanisms, national governments, humanitarian organisations, and individual initiatives, the rights of each and every individual can be maintained. Although cooperation at the highest collective level is undoubtedly key to the realisation of this credo, crucial also is the role of the individual.

---

* For full transcript of this speech see www.ucc.ie/en/ccjhr/

In a policy that may be termed the democratisation of justice, Navi Pillay advocates 'the right of survivors to participate in the justice process, directly or through legal representatives, by presenting their views and concerns at all stages to the court proceedings.' This notion of victim participation is widely recognised and lauded by human rights activists now, but it has taken the better part of the twentieth century, since the proclamation of the Universal Declaration of Human Rights in 1948, for this goal to be (partially) realised. One of the UK's most respected and charismatic human rights lawyers, Geoffrey Robertson, identified this focus on individual victims as the sustaining force in the global human rights campaign: 'There is one experience, however, which I believe all who have made a difference in human rights have in common: they have drawn their inspiration – in fact, their passion – from involvement with victims of human rights abuses. ... It is through empathy with the victim, recognising the nobility of their will to survive and their determination to overcome suffering, that the dedicated idealism for effective human rights work will be forged.'*

Perhaps Navi Pillay's early life in apartheid South

---

* Geoffrey Robertson, 'So You Want To Be A Human Rights Lawyer?' http://www.geoffreyrobertson.com/human_right_lawyer. htm

Africa affords her this ability to empathise with the victims, but uncovering the source of her dedicated idealism is trickier. Through the years Navi has displayed an extraordinary determination and capacity for endurance, coupled with a practical competence which makes her uniquely suited for her current position as the world's foremost human rights monitor.

Due to this combination of practical know-how and grit, her credo on international law and human rights also underscores national and international cooperation – what she calls the 'exchange of jurisprudence', the protection of victims and witnesses, gender sensitivity, and reparation for victims. In short, for Navi, retributive justice is not enough. Restorative justice in the form of reparation for victims is what Navi demands. Navi describes one such intervention which led to the victims of genocide in Rwanda receiving anti-retroviral medication: 'When I was President of the ICTR, I addressed a letter to the UN Secretary-General on behalf of the judges and in response to complaints from Rwandans of injustice. Rwandans at one stage called a boycott of the Tribunal and were particularly aggrieved that the Tribunal was providing HIV/Aids anti-retroviral medication to detainees in its custody, whereas victims of the genocide were not receiving any aid or treatment. We requested the UN to remedy the gap in the Statute, and make provision for compensation for victims.'

What this anecdote also reveals is that when riled enough, Navi Pillay will take on the very arbiters of human rights, as well as state tyranny, warlords, mass murderers and so on, whatever their faction or affiliation, and with very real results.

Office of the High Commissioner for Human Rights (OHCHR)

On 1 September 2008 Navi Pillay took up her position as the first African United Nations High Commissioner for Human Rights. She had been nominated by the UN Secretary-General Ban Ki-Moon, and the decision had been approved by the 192-member UN General Assembly. There were, however, detractors. The USA, then still led by George W. Bush and the Republicans, raised reservations about the nomination of Navi Pillay who was regarded as a strong supporter of abortion. Navi had always been candid about her championing of women's reproductive rights, and at this juncture, her convictions almost cost her the post of High Commissioner. The more conservative US media groups dubbed Navi the 'abortion advocate' and highlighted her association with Equality Now, which they alleged had spearheaded campaigns for abortion access in Poland and Nepal. Further claims were made about Equality Now receiving funding from pro-abortion foundations, such as the George Soros Open Society Institute and the Ford Foundation. But when the UN General Assembly came to vote, the nomination was approved by a clear majority. This negative press by factions opposed to some of her firmly-held principles was perhaps a foretaste of the challenges to come, and served only to fortify her resolve.

Gone were the plans for a quiet retirement in Durban – she was now based at the OHCHR which has its headquarters in Geneva and an office in New York. The OHCHR also has eight regional offices and ten country offices. The OHCHR is composed of four main divisions: the Human Rights Council and Treaties Division; the Special Procedures Division; the Field Operations and Technical Cooperation Division; and the Research and Right to Development Division. As indicated by the structure, the mandate of the OHCHR is complex. In addition to supporting the UN's various human rights mechanisms (in particular the UN Human Rights Council which is an inter-governmental body made up of forty-seven states), and providing a forum for discussion of human rights issues, the OHCHR coordinates work in the field, research and education projects, and the dissemination of public information. The OHCHR lists as its priorities: tackling impunity for perpetrators of human rights crimes; poverty; discrimination;

armed conflict and violence; and the lack of democracy and weak institutions. The ambit of the OHCHR is mind-bogglingly huge, involving interventions at the level of international treaties to specific peace missions and responses to human rights emergencies. What then did Navi Pillay make of her gargantuan task when she stepped into her capacious office at Palais Wilson, overlooking Lake Geneva?

Treacherous Waters

The post of High Commissioner was established in 1993 'to promote and protect the effective enjoyment by all people of all civil, cultural, economic, political and social rights, including the right to development.'* The appointment is made by the Secretary-General of the UN and is then approved by the General Assembly which gives the post its mandate: 'The High Commissioner should function as the UN official with principal responsibility for global human rights efforts.' Since the inception of the post there have been five High Commissioners, of which three have been female, suggesting that in the arena of human rights activism at this senior level, parity

---

* http://www.ohchr.org/EN/AboutUs/Pages/HighCommissioner.aspx

between the sexes has been achieved. It is a position which carries with it great moral weight, influential power, and personal honour.

But this is not a job to be coveted lightly. The responsibilities and tasks are enormous, requiring a mind like a computer to process constantly evolving data, a media-friendly personality, and scrupulous diplomatic skills. The High Commissioner has to attend the UN Human Rights Council meetings, as well as various meetings of the numerous committees and commissions of the OHCHR, issue press releases, convene conferences which bring together international dignitaries, visit regional offices of the OHCHR, and oversee the day-to-day running of the OHCHR – all of this with the knowledge that individual lives may be at stake or that an international political fracas may erupt if she treads on high-ranking toes. But this is not all that Navi faced when she accepted this onerous albeit prestigious job. With the territory come other hazards. Less than a year after he was appointed High Commissioner for Human Rights, Brazilian Sergio Vieira de Mello took a temporary leave of absence from his post to serve in Iraq as Kofi Annan's Special Representative. On 19 August 2003 Vieira de Mello and twenty-two colleagues were killed when the United Nations headquarters in Baghdad was bombed. There are member states of the Human Rights Council and diverse political factions which do not always perceive the UN as an impartial mediator of peace and human rights. Thus the UN's most high-profile human rights representative, the High Commissioner, sits on the frontline (sometimes literally) between the UN and its detractors, and has to fend off attacks and criticisms from divergent parties hell-bent on promoting their own agendas.

Navi Pillay's predecessor, Louise Arbour of Canada, did not seek a second term of office when her four-year tenure ended in 2008. Her tenure had been marred by vociferous criticism of what was perceived as her anti-Israel stance during the Israel-Lebanon conflict of 2006. Most of the criticism hurled at Arbour originated from UN Watch, a non-governmental organisation devoted to eradicating what it regards as anti-Semitism and an anti-Israel bias at the UN. A year after taking up the post Navi expressed her view on what is no doubt the most pressing challenge of the job: 'I also had to develop diplomatic skills fairly quickly, which is very different from my previous position as a judge. I've come to realise that diplomacy, quiet negotiation and cooperation from member states is key to overcoming the challenges of human rights abuses around the world.'* Although

---

* Zohra Mohammed Teke, 'I Miss Avocados and Mealie Meal' in *The Daily News*, 12 October 2009, p.9.

the High Commissioner's role is mainly one of advocacy, Navi had stepped into a political quagmire which would bring her head-to-head with the world's superpowers and some of the UN's strongest dissenters.

Added to this, her battles for justice and human rights were no longer fought in a court of law. The OHCHR, in most respects, is a watchdog, and its effective strength lies in its ability to make informed recommendations about the implementation of human rights law. Much of Navi's work now is political and depends on the cooperation and goodwill of states. No longer a prosecutor or a judge, she is now the world's moral barometer on human rights issues. In effect, she has the authority to name and shame human rights violators, often expressing vociferous condemnations, but paradoxically she has to do so with impartiality. In Navi this paradox is resolved because, over the years, experience has taught her to marry the empathy she feels with rationality and practical purpose. In her personal and professional life, Navi has learned that caring is not enough, if not met with disciplined action. In an interview with leading South African journalist and television personality, Devi Sankaree Govender, Navi attempted to explain the dual nature of her unique proficiency: 'I think that my judicial experience qualifies me to be impartial and independent, and then I come with my heart for victims all over the world because I suffered as a victim in apartheid South Africa.'*

One anecdote shared by Navi goes further towards explaining how she is able to realise the aphorism 'justice tempered with mercy' in her everyday work life. Navi tells of how, when she was working at the ICTR, she was once involved in negotiations with representatives of the Burundi government. Present also was Archbishop Desmond Tutu of South Africa. Tutu extolled the virtues of the Truth and Reconciliation Commission, which he claimed, chuckling all the time, was far more cost-efficient than an ad hoc court of law and which actually got to the truth. 'You cleanse your soul and forgive and you get on with it,' he concluded. Navi, who was sitting next to him, leaned over and said, 'Oh, you've almost convinced me.' The Archbishop replied, 'No, no, no, you carry on with the work you are doing because it is so very important.' On reflection Navi believes she learned a very valuable lesson from that sotto voce conversation: the criminal justice of the law court and the reconciliation and indemnity of the TRC are complementary processes. Both are needed if human rights are to prevail.

Now Navi Pillay is working harder than ever with

---

* Devi Sankaree Govender, *Carte Blanche* interview, 26 October 2008.

her head and her heart. Meeting her in person in June 2009, it was immediately apparent from her dignified and determined demeanour that drowning in the treacherous waters of international politicking was not an option – she remains indefatigable in her quest to champion human rights for all.

The First Year

During an hour-long interview Navi's voice remained carefully modulated and relaxed, even playful. She talked candidly about her early life and childhood, and was happy to facilitate access to the various divisions of the OHCHR. At one point she nipped out of her office to join a birthday celebration for a colleague, pausing briefly in the corridor to throw me another titbit about her past, before sanguinely dropping in on a committee meeting. Colleagues too were upbeat and helpful, taking the time to explain the internal mechanics of the OHCHR. The Director of the Human Rights Council and Treaties Division, Bacre Ndiaye, enthusiastically described the innovative process known as the Universal Periodic Review (UPR). This review is a state-driven process which analyses the human rights records of all 192 members of the UN. Echoing the optimism of their 'boss', the staff of the OHCHR I interviewed all declared the 'promising potential' of the UPR which has reviewed eighty states since its inception. When Devi Sankaree Govender asked Navi Pillay about the controversy the UPR had triggered, her answer was typically animated and forthright: 'Yes. That's a reality. Many states that we are not going to name are very reluctant to have a transparent exposure of their human rights record. So, what? Do we just sit back and do nothing about it? Or do we support an international forum where everybody, including those reluctant states, will undergo this universal review by their peers? It's a way of checking upon the record of those states you mentioned.'* Everyone at the OHCHR is affected by Navi's no-nonsense approach. Their firecracker of a boss may speak uncomfortable truths but she buoys up her team with her fearlessness and candour. However, somewhere beneath this efficient and cheerful ambience, lurk the expected tensions of an international office engaged with some of the world's most grave and intractable problems.

On 14 September 2009 Navi presented a review of her first year in office to the Human Rights Council. In this speech she refers to these problems as 'thematic priorities' of the OHCHR. Whilst reiterating to the Human Rights Council that a great deal of

---

* Devi Sankaree Govender, *Carte Blanche* interview, 26 October 2008.

decisive action was still required to deal with discrimination, violent conflict, the imbalance between the rich and the poor, illegal migrants, the suppression of free speech, and democratic deficits, Navi also pointed out the achievements of the OHCHR. The Durban Review Conference saw member states renewing their commitment to combating racism, racial discrimination, xenophobia and related intolerance. The outcome document of the conference which was endorsed by 192 states is a remarkable feat, despite the fact that the conference was boycotted by some leading nations, and present at the conference were divisive factions who seemed intent on railroading proceedings. In her review speech to the Human Rights Council, Navi also mentioned the adoption of the *Optional Protocol to the International Covenant on Economic, Social, and Cultural Rights* by the UN General Assembly. This Protocol signifies a step towards redressing the imbalances between rich and poor which have been exacerbated by the global economic crisis. Another positive outcome for Navi during this first year is the Democratic Republic of Congo's adoption of a zero tolerance policy against sexual violence.

Nevertheless, evident in this speech also is that underlying tension discernible in the corridors of the Palais Wilson. Whether referring to such human rights concerns as the sentencing of political opposition leader Aung Sang Suu Kyi to a further period of house arrest by the Myanmar authorities, or the elections in Afghanistan, the High Commissioner's speech is infused with a tone of entreaty and thinly-veiled desperation. Individual governments are extolled to address their respective human rights crises, and member states of the Human Rights Council are implored to work towards a shared purpose to ensure its credibility. Navi's rhetoric is compelling: 'This body should be prepared to confront violations wherever and whenever they take place. A failure to rise to this challenge would constitute a betrayal of the victims of human rights violations all over the world who place faith in the United Nations and, in particular, the Human Rights Council.'

She backs up these urgent appeals with examples of lassitude on the part of member states: 'A key step in the right direction would be to give effect to the International Convention on the Protection of the Rights of All Migrant Workers and Members of Their Families. The low level of acceptance of this crucial international instrument is deeply disturbing and an indication that we are not addressing this concern seriously.'*

Hearing this keynote address delivered on the occasion of her first anniversary in office, one cannot

---

* For transcripts of speeches see OHCHR official website http://www.ohchr.org/EN/Pages/WelcomePage.aspx

help but share her sense of anxiety and desperation. The world is witness to ongoing human rights abuses whilst new crises spring up every day. Only the relentless faith and effort of individuals such as Navi offer a glimmer of hope that wrongs will be righted, perpetrators punished, and victims recompensed.

2008 was the year to honour such individuals. Just four months after taking up the post at the OHCHR, Navi had the privilege of celebrating, with the rest of the UN, the sixtieth anniversary of the Universal Declaration of Human Rights (UDHR) on 10 December 2008. For most of the year, the UN had coordinated events to commemorate the occasion. These events were intended to include all branches of the UN, the public and private sectors, media, students, artists, and other representatives of civil society. Conferences and exhibitions were held, competitions were run, and media campaigns were launched. The regional offices of the OHCHR in Bangkok, Nepal, Timor-Leste, the former Yugoslav Republic of Macedonia, Azerbaijan, Georgia, Côte d'Ivoire, Guatemala, Mexico and Palestine organised commemorative events to both celebrate the UDHR and foster human rights activities in their respective regions. The OHCHR, in collaboration with a non-governmental organisation, Art of the World, ambitiously commissioned a series of short films by internationally acclaimed filmmakers and artists. The project, known as Stories on Human Rights, also features an associated book which includes work by five Nobel Prize winners, and posters designed by art students from twenty countries. The project is inspired by six inter-related themes arising from the UDHR: culture; development; dignity and justice; environment; gender; and participation. The twenty-two short films of the series are in turn shocking, thought-provoking, poignant, informative, and all are deeply pertinent.

This commemorative material comprising of posters and films (with their accompanying stories and texts) is not just celebratory but also functions as a highly effective pedagogic tool. This is perhaps due to the artistic quality of the material, but also to the fact that no high-handed editing or interfering propaganda machine is discernible in the fruits of the project. But lest anyone forget the reality on the ground in the midst of the sixtieth anniversary celebrations, Navi Pillay issued this statement to the UN General Assembly on 10 December 2008: 'Eleanor Roosevelt said, "Where, after all, do universal human rights begin? ... In small places, close to home." Until these rights touch the lives of every man, woman and child everywhere, our work is not done.'*

---

* OHCHR 2008 Report: Activities and Results, p.7.

Keeping the Faith

Certainly, Navi's work is not done. Her unswerving and sometimes frustrating campaign for human rights for all continues, but her punishing schedule is tempered with visits to her beloved South Africa where she can unwind in the company of her family and close circle of friends. Sometimes these trips home are for official reasons. On 10 December 2009, Human Rights Day, Navi was awarded an Honorary Doctorate from the University of Pretoria. Pretoria is a jacaranda-filled city in the north-east of South Africa and historically it has served as: the capital of the South African Republic when the Boers* first settled in the area in the nineteenth century; the administrative capital of the Union of South Africa when Boer territories united with the British colonies in 1910; the administrative capital when South Africa became a republic in 1961. Today it is one of South Africa's three capital cities and is the site of Nelson Mandela's momentous inauguration as president in 1994. But its former history, its iconic Union Buildings, and its infamous Voortrekker Monument† are closely associated with the apartheid regime as this was where the white minority government officially sat. But on 10

---

* See Glossary of Terms
† See Glossary of Terms

December 2009 Navi Pillay, the woman who began her life just as that iniquitous regime was taking root, was in Pretoria to receive a superlative personal accolade. She was also there to witness graduates of the Master's Degree Programme in Human Rights and Democratisation in Africa receive their honours. If ever there was a symbolic occasion this was it.

Navi's early life in South Africa had been dogged by racial and gender discrimination but now she was being applauded by a multicultural South African audience, and by the young graduates at the ceremony who had come from many states in Africa to study human rights and democracy, here in Pretoria, the former stronghold of the apartheid government. In her keynote address at this momentous event, Navi stressed the importance of embracing diversity and the equally urgent need to stamp out discrimination. It was immediately apparent that Navi was not going to offer a facile celebratory invocation to the 'new South Africa'. She reminded the audience of the widespread destruction which arises from discrimination and was bold enough to point out South Africans' xenophobia towards foreign nationals as an example. She took the opportunity to pledge her support to the South African Human Rights Commission and to praise Africans for drafting The African Charter on Human and Peoples' Rights which she cites as 'one of Africa's pioneering instruments and a pivotal contribution to the advancement of international human rights.'* As can be expected, Navi does not hold her punches, and in the same breath, she praised these advancements while exhorting Africans to bridge the gap between abstract principles and implementation on the ground.

When at home in South Africa, it is not all rest and relaxation for Navi. She is besieged by journalists wanting to interview her about her international role, but more specifically, the South African public is curious as to the High Commissioner's view on South Africa's human rights record. Navi's perspective on this subject stretches back to the 1960s, and in the 1990s just prior to her departure for Tanzania, she was directly involved in shaping the new constitution and drafting legislation for the protection of victims of domestic violence, specifically the *Domestic Violence Act* (1998). Being a central figure in the international human rights arena does not however mean that Navi Pillay is not keeping tabs on the situation in South Africa. In an interview in 2008, she commented on the efficacy of the Constitutional Court in South Africa: 'I can see lots of conflict and tension between the central and provincial legislative

---

* For transcripts of speeches see OHCHR official website http://www.ohchr.org/EN/Pages/WelcomePage.aspx

authorities and tension between genders, the diverse cultures.'*

This dissatisfaction with the implementation of South Africa's exemplary constitution was reiterated more recently when South African delegates at the UN objected to a resolution on discriminatory laws against women. Navi expressed her shock and dismay at this objection and went on to declare: 'I am anxiously watching developments in South Africa, and although we have these wonderful institutions of the judiciary and a vibrant civil society, the government needs to do more to educate its citizens on the principles of the constitution, while the recent attacks on foreigners have proved that the principles of equality are also not being observed.'†

True to her credo, the abstract principles of justice are not enough for Navi. The national government of her homeland too comes under attack when she spots a lapse in the implementation of those principles at basic and real levels.

In most of her official reprimands in her first year in office it is apparent that what Navi is pushing for is the *realisation* of human rights. Her life's work has

---

* Liz Clarke, 'Advancing Women's Status in Law' in *The Daily News*, 22 July 2008, p.9.
† Zohra Mohammed Teke, 'SA Must Show Leadership on Human Rights Issues' in *The Daily News*, 12 October 2009, p.9.

never been on an abstract, intellectual level and this is perhaps what affords her the clout to make the denouncements she does on almost a daily basis. Navi has to be careful to strike a balance between this sort of admonishment and the upbeat praise and congratulations she offered to the youthful graduates at the University of Pretoria. With meticulous diplomatic skill, the High Commissioner has to take governments to task when human rights are violated, but at the same time it is her responsibility to help individual citizens keep the faith.

Detractors accuse the High Commissioner of failing to act decisively against governments. There have been suggestions that the OHCHR needs more powers to compel governments to act on their recommendations. After reflecting on the mandate of the OHCHR and considering at some length the individual who heads this organisation, it seems that the power of the High Commissioner, however, is not political in nature, but rather it belongs to the realm of morality and justice. Navi *does* have the power to stand up and be heard when she makes a speech about the failures of international and national law to protect individuals from discrimination and abuse. In some instances, when she does so, she may be branded a Tamil Tiger stooge or an anti-Israeli campaigner. Such name-calling is very unlikely to cow Navi from appealing for the rights of dissidents in Sri

Lanka or from demanding the end to impunity for human rights violaters in the Occupied Palestinian Territory. These red flags will go unheeded as Navi is no raging bull. Her sights are fervently and firmly set on tackling ongoing battles such as widespread and blatant discrimination against women.

In her speech in Pretoria, Navi returned to a topic which has in the past both greatly distressed her, and strongly galvanised her into action: 'Despite significant improvements over the past century, women and girls are still discriminated against to some degree in all societies and to a great degree in many. Every day countless numbers of women are sexually or physically abused. In the vast majority of cases, their tormentors go unpunished, and future abuse is undeterred. Women work two-thirds of the world's working hours and produce half of the world's food, yet earn only ten per cent of the world's income and own less than one per cent of the world's property. They continue to suffer the worst forms of economic discrimination even though they are a dynamic, productive source of economic development.'*

Navi's counsel in response to such discrimination is, in the first instance, to prevail upon states to live up to their international obligations, and then, for

---

* For transcripts of speeches see OHCHR official website http:// www.ohchr.org/EN/Pages/WelcomePage.aspx

national governments to use the law to eradicate discriminatory customs, practices and prejudices. For Navi the implementation of the law 'is an indispensable starting point for the creation of a level playing field.'* The individual too has an obligation and here Navi advocates looking to shared cultural values and traditions for moral guidance. This may seem like a u-turn for someone who herself has never been circumscribed by convention, but Navi learned a great deal about a society which has lost its moral compass when she worked at the ICTR. She strongly believes that individuals can be deterred from infringing on the human rights of another if pride in one's own culture is fostered alongside tolerance of other cultures. Not exactly a conformist herself, Navi nevertheless is of the view that adherence to what is best in her own cultural heritage is what has kept her so strongly grounded all these years.

The future then is mapped out for this extraordinary woman. As long as such human rights abuses continue, she will advocate that international and national human rights be employed to bring about redress. She has come a long way since defending indigent farmers in KwaZulu-Natal or running an advice desk for abused women from her home, but

---

* Devi Sankaree Govender, *Carte Blanche* interview, 26 October 2008.

her faith in inalienable rights and the potential efficacy of judicial systems has remained steady. With
three more years to serve as UN High Commissioner
for Human Rights, she will no doubt continue to be,
in her words, 'the voice of victims everywhere'.

Conclusion

AT SOME POINT EVERY PERSON contemplates what meaning their life holds. Some hope to find enlightenment, others hope for fame or riches, or still others long for just a free and peaceful existence. A few are blessed with a purpose which makes amply clear the meaning of their time on this earth. Navi Pillay is one of those few who have made it their life's task to help other people. Her work, spanning five decades, has focused on the rights of those who are most vulnerable and traumatised. Her mantra has remained steadfast – use the rule of the law to achieve, in real terms, human rights for all. But the path to her current position, where this philosophy is being realised, has been a bumpy one.

She almost did not gain entrance to school. A dignified and determined mother, a woman with humble ambitions and a deep respect for the power of education, saw to it that her gifted daughter got the opportunity which was her right. She almost did not obtain a tertiary education because her bus-driver father could not afford the university fees. A prescient school principal and a supportive community came to the rescue, recognising that an exceptional talent should not be wasted. She almost did not find employment because she was a black, working-class woman in 1960s South Africa. By this stage Navi was a feisty, self-possessed, and industrious woman. She simply created her own employment by opening a law firm. From then on, with the precedent set, it has been one singular victory or accomplishment after another, leading eventually to the Palais Wilson in Geneva.

What accounts for this extraordinary record: the exceptional circumstances of her early life in apartheid South Africa; the nurturing of strong and indomitable parents; personal will and remarkable intelligence; or selflessness and a lofty moral code? The answer, surely, is the sum of these parts. Navi's life combines extraordinary circumstances with extraordinary innate qualities.

Surprising is this great woman's down-to-earth manner. Yes, she can be commanding or imposing when she requires it and she oozes self-confidence and dignity, but she is also self-deprecatory when it comes to compliments and dismissive when her humble beginnings are too closely analysed. As far as she is concerned, the media makes too much of her past and she sees herself as just one of millions of disenfranchised

South Africans at the time. She is equally matter-of-fact about her outstanding intellect, recalling quite casually that she spent her spare time at university reading the records of the Nuremberg Trials. While other students were no doubt engaged in more sociable activities, Navi found a quiet corner to read these historic documents and contemplate how such legal ideas may be applied in the South African context. Yet, she believes that she is an ordinary person.

This image of the studious undergraduate with grave ambitions may be misleading. Navi has always been warm, empathetic and fun-loving. In photos from the 1960s and 1970s she is seen striding through the streets of Durban with her husband Gaby, both cutting dashing figures in their crisp fashions and their camaraderie immediately evident. Other photos show her smiling with her arms around her young daughters or the family dog, clad in a sari, lolling in the garden, looking as if she did not have a care in the world. Her daughter Kamini describes how Navi has always been a 'dog person'. Over the years Navi has had Dobermans, Pomeranians and German Shepherds. But it is no secret that her favourite dog has always been a mongrel named Ringo (after Ringo Starr). Ringo was Navi and Gaby's darling before the girls came along, and apparently, to this day Navi claims that no other dog can ever match up to the lofty standards set by her beloved Ringo.

There is then, at the heart of this powerhouse, a joyful exuberance and zest for life which defies analysis, considering the iniquities she has experienced firsthand and as a judge. This warmth is most evident in her private life but spills over into her professional realm too.

For rest and relaxation Navi reads, and reads, and reads … When she can manage it, she visits the theatre but her recreational activity of choice is definitely reading. She reads voraciously anything she can lay her hands on, but not surprisingly news and current affairs form part of her daily literary diet. It is perhaps a little known fact that Navi is a keen golfer. Her busy schedule means she does not get onto the golf course as often as she would like, and like the source of her boundless energy, her handicap remains a mystery. She unwinds also by walking in the countryside, or, when she can entice opponents to take her on, by playing Scrabble. Her family rather nervously testifies to her passion for board games, perhaps because she inevitably wins every game.

Navi is always immaculately groomed and at sixty-eight she is still a strikingly attractive woman. She developed a unique personal flair long before the media spotlights turned their gaze on her. Her sense of style is eclectic. Her shopping habits reflect her variegated life experiences. She will pick up a garment in a European fashion house and team it with accessories from a bargain basement in New York or ethnic African jewellery to create a look which is both chic and fitting for her venerable role. Whatever the provenance of her ensemble, she always exudes elegance and self-assurance, mingled with a faint trace of Chanel perfume.

On her sixtieth birthday she was inundated with wishes and tributes, not least of all from her family, and her colleagues at the time from the International Criminal Tribunal in Rwanda. With every passing year, Navi receives more and more adulation and homage from those who know her and from strangers. For this is the woman who finds time to attend a party or cook meals for her colleagues, in between hearing the testimony of mass murderers or castigating national governments for reneging on their human rights pledges.

Her unpretentious, modest manner has won her many admirers across the world. When she lived in Arusha, she eschewed the practice common amongst her colleagues at the TRC of renting a lavish home and employing an army of servants. Navi refused to exploit the cheap labour force available to her with her UN-funded salary. At the moment in Geneva she rents a simple apartment when she could easily afford one of the luxury properties on the shoreline of Lake Geneva. With her family, though, she is extremely generous with her time and her money. If she cannot slip away from her work commitments to visit them, she arranges for them to fly to where she is. In July 2009 when she found herself bound to her duties over the summer months, Kamini and Isvari, and grandson Sendhil joined her for a low-key holiday in Geneva. Her siblings are deeply grateful that she has never neglected them, however arduous her schedule. As sister, mother, grandmother, aunt, her record is as impressive as her professional one.

To look at her smooth, smiling face one would never guess that she has been exposed to countless harsh and terrifying experiences. She has been under surveillance by the South African Special Branch, she has been witness to the unlawful detention of both husband and close friends, and she has listened to graphic accounts of some of the most heinous and vicious crimes. How does she retain her faith in humanity after having watched video footage of pregnant women being disembowelled? Navi's answer to this question is simple – she believes her training as a judge is what affords her the mettle to look at the darkest side of human nature, and then to withdraw in order to focus on what good can be done. In Navi's case good works are achieved through belief in the principle of justice. Yet, the ability to focus positively on this principle rather than slump into the depths of despair, or even depression if the experience is repeated, cannot be pinned down by science or reason. In a person like Navi this belief sits alongside a probing intellect, she has faith but she is not complacent.

Navi was, after all, the six-year-old girl who stood in a High Court and gave evidence against her father's colleague. When the case ended she was left asking 'Where is my father's money, is this justice?' She still questions the tenets of justice. The difference is that now she is sixty-eight years old, the UN High Commissioner for Human Rights, with a long and illustrious career behind her. Her question today has therefore been modified to include all of humanity: 'Where is justice for each and every one of us?' All her life she had enquired, believed, and moreover, she has answered with action, not just words.

Her life-long quest for justice has won her enemies too, those who would belittle her efforts or criticise her methods, although the ideals she adheres to may be harder to fault. Of course, not everyone shares Navi's convictions, and when it comes to controversial topics such as abortion, there is bound to be mudslinging. Along the way there have been setbacks, failures, disappointments, and sometimes heartache. None of these, just as none of the adversaries, has ever proved to be an obstacle.

As for the future, anything is possible for the woman who says that nothing but physical infirmity will cause her to retire from public service. After all,

Navi appreciates that history unravels in surprising and ironic ways. Who would have thought that Jan Smuts, a white supremacist, would leave the preamble to the UN charter as his lasting legacy to the world? Who would have believed in 1963 that Nelson Mandela would one day be president of South Africa and a global icon of freedom? And who would have guessed that the six-year-old who questioned the meaning of justice would one day be realising human rights for all?

Biography

23 Sep. 1941	Navanethem Pillay is born in Clairwood, Durban, South Africa to Narrainsamy Naidoo, a bus driver and Santhama Naidoo, a housewife.
1948	The Nationalist Party wins first full election victory in South Africa and apartheid is formally established. In the same year the Universal Declaration of Human Rights is drafted.
1955	Navi wins an essay competition for her essay entitled 'Why We Should Buy South African-made Goods'. She is awarded a medal instead of prize money.
1957	Navi wins a national essay competition organised by the Union of Jewish Women. The essay is entitled 'The Role of Women in South Africa'.

1958   Navi wins the Jan Hofmeyr Speech Contest and the Students Historic Society Speech Contest. For the latter she spoke on the topic: 'It Would Have Been Better for the world if Vasco Da Gama Had Never Sailed'.

1959   Attends University of Natal campus for non-whites.

1963   Obtains BA but because of the *Separate Universities Act*, she is not allowed to continue with LL.B at the University of Natal. She is told she has to transfer to the newly opened University College of Indians.

1965   After appealing to the Minister of Indian affairs, she is given special permission to continue with studies, obtains LL.B from the University of Natal.

1965–67   Internship, articled to a member of the ANC who is under banning orders.

1966   Establishes clandestine links with Amnesty International. Later she convinces Amnesty International to adopt South African prisoners. At great risk from the apartheid government's covert forces, she also sent information about prisoners and children in detention to Amnesty International.

1967   Navi is the first black women in
        South Africa to open a law practice –
        Navanethem Pillay & Company, Attorneys
        and Conveyancers.

1971   Husband, Gaby Pillay, and other members
        of New Unity Movement are detained
        under the *Terrorism Act*. Navi brings a
        successful application in court to stop
        police from using unlawful methods of
        interrogation against political prisoners.

1972   The United Nation's Subcommittee of
        the General Assembly on apartheid
        adopted Navi Pillay's 1971 application as a
        document in their collection on torture.
        Visits Robben Island when the case State
        vs Kader Hassim and Twelve Others is
        appealed. Lodges successful application for
        the rights of prisoners, including Nelson
        Mandela, on Robben Island.

1973   Daughter Isvari arrives.

1976   Daughter Kamini arrives.

1978   Acts as defense attorney for Harry Gwala,
        leader of ANC for Natal Province and
        nine other ANC members charged under
        the *Terrorism Act*. This was a long and
        complicated case. The prisoners testified to
        police torture and ill-treatment.

1979	Lost the Gwala case, all the accused were imprisoned on Robben Island. After this defeat Navi decided to expose the details of these cases to overseas legal experts.
	In June of the same year Navi's mother, Santhama Naidoo, died.
1981	Awarded a Harvard University scholarship for graduate study – LL.M degree. Began forging more international links.
1984	Returned to Harvard to study for a doctorate in juridical science.
1986	Navi founded the Advice Desk for Abused Women together with friend and colleague, Dr Anshu Padayachee.
1988	First South African to obtain a doctorate in law from Harvard Law School. Her thesis was controversially entitled 'The Political Role of the South African Judiciary'.
	Joined the Amnesty International Human Rights Now! concert tour to popularise the Universal Declaration of Human Rights.
1989	Begins lecturing at the University of Natal.
1990	On 11 February 1990 Nelson Mandela was released from prison.
	Later that year Navi's article 'The Role of a Conscientious Lawyer in the South African Legal System' was published.

1992	Co-founded the international women's rights group Equality Now with Jessica Neuwirth.
	During this period Navi worked for the National Women's Coalition and was involved in drafting South Africa's new constitution.
	Navi is elected to the Law Faculty Board and then the Council of the University of Durban-Westville.
27 April 1994	First democratic elections held in South Africa. Nelson Mandela inaugurated as president.
1995	Navi is the first black woman to be appointed as acting judge for the Supreme Court of South Africa.
	Appointed to serve as judge on Unite Nation's International Criminal Tribunal in Rwanda (ICTR). Navi left South Africa to settle in Arusha, Tanzania.
	Navi and Gaby are divorced.
1998	Sits on the bench as ICTR finds Jean Kambanda, the former prime minister of Rwanda, guilty of genocide and crimes against humanity. She is also on the bench when the ICTR sentenced former mayor Jean-Paul Akayesu for genocide and crimes against humanity, and for other

violations including rape and encouraging widespread sexual violence. This landmark verdict held that rape had been used as an act of genocide, as well as an act of torture. Both cases set precedents in international criminal law.

1999   Elected as the ICTR's first woman president.

2003   Joined the Appeals Division of the International Criminal Court at The Hague. Navi relocated to the Netherlands.

2006   Navi's father, Narrainsamy Naidoo died, aged 100.

2008   Appointed as United Nations High Commissioner for Human Rights. Navi makes Geneva, Switzerland her home. This year was also the sixtieth anniversary of the Universal Declaration of Human Rights.

Glossary of Terms

Black: In this biography the word black is used as an umbrella term to denote all the peoples of South Africa, through the ages, who have been oppressed or racially discriminated against by the white minority population. The indigenous African people of the region are referred to as black Africans.

Coolie: The term 'coolie' is derived from the Tamil word *kuli* which referred to the lowest of menial workers. British colonials used the term as a generalising, demeaning marker of subjection for all Indians

Satyagraha: This term is comprised of two Sanskrit words (*satya* which means 'truth' and *agraha* which means 'to hold firmly to'). It is a form of non-violent resistance developed by Mahatma Gandhi during his stay in South Africa. The theory and philosophy of *satyagraha* have influenced many revolutionaries and dissidents, including Nelson Mandela and Martin Luther King Junior.

Coloured: The term 'coloured' is used in South Africa to denote a category of people who are historically of mixed race, the result of miscegenation between the Dutch settlers and indigenous peoples during the seventeenth and eighteenth centuries.

Ramayana and *Bhagavad Gita*: The *Ramayana* is a Sanskrit epic poem dating from about 750 BC which has great religious and cultural influence in South Asia. It depicts the trials and tribulations of the virtuous hero, Rama (an incarnation of the Hindu god Vishnu), his wife Sita (the incarnation of Lakshmi) and the Hanuman (the incarnation of Shiva). The *Bhagavad Gita* is the principle religious text of the Hindu faith. It takes the form of an edifying conversation between Krishna and Arjuna on the battlefield and is considered by scholars to be one of the world's greatest literary and philosophical texts.

Special Branch: The South African Police Service's Special Branch spied on, detained or attacked anti-government political activists – those deemed 'enemies of the state'. Detainees were often tortured whilst in police custody. During the apartheid decades thousands of activists were murdered or 'disappeared', never to be seen again. Many others went into exile to escape the brutality of the Special Branch.

Kala pani: The term literally means black water in Hindi, and has its origins in Indian superstitions about the sea and its dangers. Since colonial times and the implementation of the indenture system the term has come to signify the fear felt by indentured labourers that their ties to the motherland would be severed if they crossed the seas.

Diwali (or Deepavali): the Hindu festival of lights which celebrates the triumph of good over evil or light over darkness. The notion is derived from the story of Rama's banishment from his home and subsequent return, as set out in the *Ramayana*.

Orange Free State: Since 1994 the Orange Free State (named after the Dutch royal family, the House of Orange) is called the Free State. This province was once a Boer Republic where Dutch was the official language until it was annexed by the British in 1900 during the Anglo-Boer War (mainly because of its diamond mines). It remained a predominantly Afrikaans province and the apartheid laws were even more stringent here than the rest of the country.

Geneva Conventions: These conventions are made up of four treaties and three protocols which outline the rights of the victims of war according to international law. These conventions were negotiated after World War Two and have been ratified, sometimes wholly and sometimes partially, by 194 nations.

Boers: Historically this is a term used to denote a Dutch settler in South Africa. Literally the term means farmer and in more recent times it has been used to refer derogatively to Afrikaners.

Voortrekker Monument: This is a massive granite monument just outside Pretoria which commemorates the Afrikaners who left the Cape Colony in the mid-nineteenth century to escape British control. It is both a symbol of pride and heritage for the Afrikaners of South Africa, and a reminder of the white minority's oppression of the black majority for 350 years.

Bibliography

Books and Articles

Bouvard, Marguerite G. *Women Reshaping Human Rights: How Extraordinary Activists Are Changing the World*. Wilmington, Delaware: SR Books, 1996.

Chetty, Sharon. 'Durban's Navi and the Rock Superstars' in *The Sunday Times Extra*, 6 November 1988.

Clarke, Liz. 'Advancing Women's Status in Law' in *The Daily News*, 22 July 2008.

Conrad, Joseph. *Heart of Darkness*. London: WW Norton and Company, 1988.

Desai, Ashwin and Vahed, Goolam. *Inside Indenture: A South African Story, 1860–1914*. Durban: Madiba Publishers, 2007.

Eboe-Osuji, Chile. 'Navi Pillay in Her Age: An Introduction' in *Protecting Humanity in the Age of Navi: Essays* [publication pending].

Goonam K. *Coolie Doctor – An Autobiography by Dr Goonam*. Durban: Madiba Publications, 1991.

Govender, Devi Sankaree. *Carte Blanche* interview, 26 October 2008.

Halstead, Peter. *The Facts At Your Fingertips … Human Rights*. London: Hodder Education, 2008.

Horner, Brett. 'A Matter of Life and Death' in *Sunday Tribune News*, 1 February 2004.

Jaichand, Vinodh. 'Navi Pillay: Overcoming the Odds' in Chile Eboe-Osuji (ed.), *Protecting Humanity in the Age of Navi: Essays* [publication pending].

Kallaway, Peter (ed.). *Apartheid and Education: The Education of Black South Africans*. Ohio: Ohio University Press, 1985.

Kuppusami, C. 'A Short History of Indian Education' in *Fiat Lux*, Vol 1, 1 May 1966.

Mandela, Nelson. 'Freedom in our Lifetime' in *Liberation,* newspaper of the Congress Movement, June 1956.

Mohammed Teke, Zohra. 'I Miss Avocados and Mealie Meal ' in *The Daily News*, 12 October 2009.

Mohammed Teke, Zohra. 'SA Must Show Leadership on Human Rights Issues' in *The Daily News*, 12 October 2009.

Møse, Erik. 'On the Bench with Navi' in Chile Eboe-Osuji (ed.), *Protecting Humanity in the Age of Navi: Essays* [publication pending].

Ngotezi, Alfred. 'We Neither Target Nor Favour Any Groups in Rwanda' in *The East African*, 20 March 2000.

Nichols, John. 'She's Called "My Lord"' in *The Natal Witness*, 28 February 1995.

Neuwirth, Jessica. 'Navi Pillay: Up Close and Personal' in Chile Eboe-Osuji (ed.), *Protecting Humanity in the Age of Navi: Essays* [publication pending].

Office of the High Commissioner for Human Rights 2008 Report: Activities and Results.

Pillay, Charmaine. 'Judging Genocide' in *The Natal Post*, 25 June 1997.

Pillay, Navanethem. 'Equal Justice for Women: A Personal Journey' in *Arizona Law Review*, Vol 50, No. 3, Fall 2008.

Pillay, Navanethem. 'Equal Rights for Women' in *African Law Review*, 3 April 1992.

Reddy, ES. 'Defiance Campaign in South Africa, Recalled' in *Asian Times*, London, 26 June 1987.

Websites

Information on Dr Goonam based on an interview with Vanitha Chetty, daughter, conducted by Rajes Pillay on 13 June 2002. http://scnc.ukzn.ac.za/doc/Audio/VOR/GoonamK/GoonamKlTranscript.htm

Voices of Resistance: Dr K. Goonam compiled by K. Chetty http://scnc.ukzn.ac.za/doc/Audio/VOR/GoonamK/GoonamKbackground.htm

George Houser: 'The International Impact of the South African Struggle for Liberation.' http://www.anc.org.za/ancdocs/history/misc/hous123.html

For a full transcript of the Nelson Mandela's speech at the Rivonia Trial see http://www.anc.org.za/ancdocs/history/rivonia.html

For speech transcripts and more information see the OHCHR official website http://www.ohchr.org/EN/Pages/WelcomePage.aspx

Geoffrey Robertson, 'So You Want To Be A Human Rights Lawyer?' http://www.geoffreyrobertson.com/human_right_lawyer.htm

For Navi Pillay's address to the Centre for Criminal Justice and Human Rights, *University of Cork, Faculty of Law see http://www.ucc.ie/en/ccjhr/.../document-2,64746,en.doc*

Acknowledgements

THERE ARE A NUMBER OF PEOPLE who have made this book possible. First, I thank Rosemarie Hudson for commissioning this work and for devising the Black-Amber Inspiration series. Our meetings at the Victoria and Albert Museum are testimony to how work and pleasure can be successfully combined. I am also grateful to the team at Arcadia Books – Gary Pulsifer, Daniela de Groote and Angeline Rothermundt – for publishing this biography. Thanks must go also to Geraldine D'Amico for suggesting, between sun salutations, that Rosemarie and I should work together. Yoga retreats have many, unexpected benefits!

The information in this biography has been gleaned from a variety of sources, but the primary source has been interviews with people who have been most generous with their time and forthcoming with their knowledge. In this regard, I am deeply indebted to High Commissioner Navi Pillay for her cooperation. She has been most gracious in facilitating this project, and interviewing her was both inspirational and a great pleasure. The staff at the Office of the High Commissioner for Human Rights have been friendly and obliging despite their busy schedules. In particular I thank Loretta Bondi, Carole Ray, Ibrahim Salama, Bacre Ndiaye, Rupert Colville and Melinda Ching.

I could not have written this biography without the input of Navi Pillay's family. Brothers, sisters, daughter, nieces, in-laws – they all welcomed me, fed me and shared their memories with me. I cannot thank them enough for taking the time and making such an enormous effort to assist. In particular, I am deeply grateful to Jenny Pillay and Kamini Pillay for providing me with important factual information, and to Pulan Naidoo for making Navi Pillay's personal archives available to me. Thank you also to Dayapushnee, Minoulee, Genanathan and Yogi for granting me interviews. Cousin, Devi Rajab, has also kindly passed on her views and anecdotes.

Navi's friends were equally helpful and enthusiastic about the project. Sonny and Theresa Venkatrathnam welcomed me into their home and Sonny relived many painful memories in order to help me. My sincere thanks to them both. Anshu Padayachee took time from her busy schedule to see me, granting me a vivacious and memorable interview.

Many others have been willing to help and share

their material. I am indebted to Devi Sankaree Govender who sent me a transcript of her television interview with Navi Pillay. Also, Chile Eboe-Osuji very generously allowed me the use of his unpublished manuscript. Thanks to him and his contributors. Natasha Naidoo at the ICC was kind enough to remember a normal day in the working life of Navi Pillay, and the stalwarts at the Union of Jewish Women of South Africa sent their very positive views.

Thanks also to Aylwyn Walsh for proof-reading the manuscript and to Brian Pearce for so enthusiastically providing useful information on Mabel Palmer.

I must also thank: my father for years of encouragement and support; Dan Wylie for being an inspiration; and Adam and Leroy for love and tolerance. If I have omitted anyone from this list, my apologies. All errors are my own.